D0948769

Protestantism and
the New South
North Carolina Baptists and
Methodists in Political Crisis
1894-1903

RK.

Protestantism and the New South

North Carolina Baptists and Methodists in Political Crisis 1894 - 1903

Frederick A. Bode

University Press of Virginia
Charlottesville

THE UNIVERSITY PRESS OF VIRGINIA
Copyright © 1975 by the Rector and Visitors
of the University of Virginia

First published 1975

Library of Congress Cataloging in Publication Data

Bode, Frederick A.   1940–
    Protestantism and the New South.

    Includes bibliographical references and index.
    1. North Carolina-Religion.   2. Protestant churches–North Carolina.   3. North Carolina–Social conditions.   I. Title.   BR555.N78B62   261.8'09756   75-1289
ISBN 0-8139-0597-4

Printed in the United States of America

For my Mother and Father

Acknowledgments

IT IS A PLEASURE to acknowledge the assistance of teachers, friends, and colleagues. Timothy H. Breen of Northwestern University and George B. Tindall and Joel Williamson of the University of North Carolina at Chapel Hill read an earlier version of the manuscript and offered useful suggestions. I am particularly grateful to Professor Williamson for his encouragement and faith in my work. The intellectual stimulation gained from conversation with Richard Roman of the University of Toronto has been of immense value. In a different form this study was submitted as a dissertation to Yale University. I would like to express my gratitude to members of my dissertation committee, Sydney E. Ahlstrom and Howard R. Lamar, and particularly to C. Vann Woodward, who not only supervised the project with patience and wise counsel but enriched my understanding of southern history in countless ways. Yale University also offered needed financial aid at crucial stages in the research. The congenial intellectual atmosphere of the Sir George Williams Department of History of Concordia University and the encouragement given by many colleagues facilitated the tedious work of revision.

The staffs of libraries and archives were generous with their time and expertise. The following institutions have kindly granted permission to quote from material in their collections: the Southern Historical Collection, University of North Carolina Library, Chapel Hill; the University of North Carolina Archives; the Duke University Library; the Duke University Archives; the Library of the University of North Carolina at Greensboro; the North Carolina State Archives; the Manuscript Division, Library of Congress; and the Harvard College Library. I also wish to thank the Southern Historical Association for permission to use as the basis for Chapter 3 and a part of the Introduction a revised version of my article, "Religion and Class Hegemony: A Populist Critique in North Carolina," *Journal of Southern History* 37 (1971): 417-38 (Copyright 1971 by the Southern Historical Association. Reprinted by permission of the Managing Editor).

My wife, Janice Joann Simpkins, shared with me both the anguish and enthusiasm of putting this study together in its final form. Those to whom this work is dedicated made it all possible.

FREDERICK A. BODE

Montreal, Quebec
April 1975

Contents

Protestantism and
the New South
North Carolina Baptists and
Methodists in Political Crisis
1894-1903

Introduction

IN HIS INFLUENTIAL STUDY of southern politics during the 1940s, V. O. Key, Jr., described North Carolina as a "Progressive Plutocracy." The state had promoted a balanced economic growth, steadily improved its educational facilities, and given little encouragement to demagogic politics and violent outbursts of racial hysteria. Largely responsible for this development, according to Key, was the pervasive influence of an "aggressive aristocracy of manufacturing and banking. . . . For half a century an economic oligarchy has held sway."[1] Though harried labor organizers and civil rights activists might offer qualifications, Key's view of North Carolina as an exception among southern states has considerable validity. In the 1920s North Carolina stood in the "forefront" of what George B. Tindall has called "business progressivism" with its programs for good roads, public health, education, and industrial development. The state was, in the words of Nell Battle Lewis, the "Wisconsin of the South."[2] In the same decade the fundamentalist antievolution crusade was notably less successful in North Carolina than in other southern states.[3] North Carolina first established its progressive reputation at the beginning of the twentieth century during the administration of Charles Brantley Aycock, the "educational governor." He came to power with a reinvigorated Democratic leadership that was closely aligned with the business community and dedicated to social stability and orderly progress.[4] At the turn of the century, however, North Carolina's "innovating elite" was

---

[1] Key, *Southern Politics in State and Nation* (New York, 1949), p. 211 and in general pp. 205-28.

[2] Tindall, *The Emergence of the New South, 1913-1945* (Baton Rouge, La., 1967), pp. 225-27.

[3] Willard B. Gatewood, *Preachers, Pedagogues, and Politicians: The Evolution Controversy in North Carolina, 1920-1927* (Chapel Hill, 1966).

[4] For a detailed account of Aycock's administration, see Oliver H. Orr, Jr., *Charles Brantley Aycock* (Chapel Hill, 1961), pp. 189-334.

not unique. It had counterparts in other southern states and in the country at large where businessmen sought to use government to promote "rational" development.[5]

In 1900 it was not entirely a foregone conclusion that the New Order would establish such deep roots in North Carolina. The soil was not fertile to begin with, and the 1890s promised anything but stability. Like its sister states in the South, North Carolina experienced during that decade a severe economic depression, the revolt of hard-pressed Populist farmers against Democratic supremacy, and an intensification of racist agitation. The Civil War and Reconstruction had destroyed a southern society with slavery and the plantation system at its base, but the shift from slave to legally free labor did not immediately spur the development of industrial capitalism. There were other serious obstacles. Interrelated with each other and all conspiring to hold the South in the vise of backwardness were a depressed agriculture characterized by tenantry and sharecropping, difficulties in accumulating local capital, the lack of a prosperous home market, parsimonious state governments, and "colonial" subordination to economic interests outside the region. Nevertheless, the death of the slave regime gave life to an ideological commitment on the part of some southerners to capitalist industrialization. These evangelists of a "New South" rejected many aspects of the old antebellum order and waxed ecstatic over the promises of "progress" in the new. But their crusade was based on a good deal of wishful thinking and mythmaking, and the 1890s saw many of their fondest hopes dashed.

North Carolina was no exception. Having little faith in the New South vision of progress, farmers came to the realization that they were at the mercy of economic forces which they, as individuals, could do little to control. In the late 1880s many joined the Farmers' Alliance, which aimed at collective economic and political action. In 1892 the discontented began to leave the "party of their fathers" for the newly organized Populist movement. Economic depression hastened the onset of revolt against Democratic

[5]Sheldon Hackney, *Populism to Progressivism in Alabama* (Princeton, N.J., 1969), pp. 329-32; C. Vann Woodward, *Origins of the New South* (Baton Rouge, La., 1951), pp. 369-95; Gabriel Kolko, *The Triumph of Conservatism: A Reinterpretation of American History, 1900-1916* (New York, 1963).

supremacy, unbroken in North Carolina since 1876. In 1894, a fusion of Populists and Republicans finally wrenched control of the state legislature from the Democrats, and in 1896 the same combination made a clean sweep of all state offices. A state historian, otherwise rather unsympathetic to Populism, had to admit in retrospect that Democratic rule had exhibited "timidity" and "lack of social responsibility"; "a rebirth was necessary and that could only come in labor and travail."[6] In the long run the Populists were unable to provide a successful ideological alternative. They were dependent on an unstable alliance with the Republicans, helpless in the face of economic problems they understood only imperfectly, and victimized by their opponents' racist demagoguery. Fusion went down to defeat in 1898. Within a resurgent Democratic party, on the other hand, businessmen as a class were able to assert that decisive role, or hegemony, in state affairs that Key and others have described.

The hegemony of any class requires not only economic power but political power; and the ability to exercise political power, if it is to have any degree of permanency and not necessitate constant repression, depends upon a broadly based ideological consensus. The concept of hegemony used here owes much to the thought of the Italian Marxist Antonio Gramsci. It may be defined as the means by which a social class maintains its domination not by force but by consent, by the active or passive acceptance by large segments of the population of ideological assumptions conducive to the stability and functioning of a social system. Hegemony depends upon the existence of a broadly based consensus that the economic organization of a society, its political framework, and the distribution of rewards and power are by and large legitimate. According to a student of Gramsci's work, hegemony is "an order in which a certain way of life and thought is dominant, in which one concept of reality is diffused throughout society in all its institutional and

[6]Joseph G. deRoulhac Hamilton, *North Carolina since 1860* (Chicago and New York, 1919), p. 218. For the southern context of North Carolina Populism, see Woodward, pp. 175-290. For the North Carolina background, see Stuart Noblin, *Leonidas Lafayette Polk, Agrarian Crusader* (Chapel Hill, 1949), pp. 190-200. An insightful critique of the New South ideology is Paul M. Gaston, *The New South Creed: A Study in Southern Mythmaking* (New York, 1970).

private manifestations, informing with its spirit all taste, morality, customs, religious and political principles, and all social relations, particularly in their institutional and moral connotation. . . . *egemonia* is the 'normal' form of [class] control, force and coercion becoming dominant only at times of crisis."[7]

This study analyzes one aspect of the transitional process during the 1890s through which New South capitalism achieved its ideological hegemony in North Carolina. It focuses on the adjustment that white Protestantism, particularly the Baptist and Methodist churches, made to the changes taking place at that time. Evangelical Protantism, both white and black, has constituted a vital part of southern culture. "As acknowledged shepherds of the Southern folds," C. Vann Woodward has written, "the Protestant clergy enjoyed a position that was unchallenged."[8] But coming to terms with the social implications of that position is not an easy problem. The social significance of religion depends upon the circumstances of a particular historical moment during which certain religious traditions interact with other variables. According to Seymour Martin Lipset, religion has been the "most common" source of values that "lead the lower strata to accept the orientation of the privileged ones." On the other hand, religion can provide the fervor for and contribute to the ideological complex of socially subversive movements of considerable importance. The role of Puritanism in the English Revolution comes to mind as an obvious example. It can also provide a sense of community and solidarity among the poor and dispossessed as it did among American slaves and even among the white working classes in the United States and elsewhere.[9]

[7]Gwyn A. Williams, "The Concept of 'Egemonia' in the Thought of Antonio Gramsci: Some Notes on Interpretation," *Journal of the History of Ideas* 21 (1960): 587, 591. The best study in English of Gramsci's political career is John M. Cammett, *Antonio Gramsci and the Origins of Italian Communism* (Stanford, Calif., 1967). See also the review essay by Eugene D. Genovese reprinted in *For a New America: Essays in History and Politics from Studies on the Left, 1959-1967,* eds. James Weinstein and David W. Eakins (New York, 1970), pp. 284-316.

[8]P. 169.

[9]Lipset, "Class, Politics, and Religion in Modern Society: The Dilemma of the Conservatives," in *Revolution and Counterrevolution: Change and Persistence in Social Structure* (rev. paperback ed.; Garden City, N.Y., 1970), p. 204. The classic attempt to relate religious values to social change is Max Weber, *The Protestant Ethic and the Spirit of Capitalism* (New York, 1958). See also Michael Walzer, *The Revolution of the Saints:*

In the South the role of religion has often been a hegemonic one, disguised though it was by the doctrine of the spiritual nature of the church. Most southern churchmen adhered at least in principle to this doctrine, which assumed a clear distinction between spiritual concerns, the province of the churches, and secular concerns, the province of politics. The churches' legitimate interest in personal morality and ethics provided the only bridge between the two realms. Good men presumably insured, or at least were necessary for, a good society. In fact, however, social and spiritual values proved inseparable. The major white Protestant denominations not only had maintained close ideological ties with the ruling classes since the antebellum period; they also had reinforced traditional values that provided a consensual basis for social stability. But in the 1890s agrarian radicalism attacked the existing distribution of economic, social, and political power and in so doing challenged many of the institutions and ideological assumptions which sustained that power. Among other things, North Carolina Populists exposed the traditional hegemonic function of the Protestant denominations. Many ministers responded with righteous indignation and clearly identified themselves with the social order the Populists were trying to change. These churchmen supported those values—white supremacy, the superiority of southern civilization, and the unique purity of southern religion—which the Democratic party had defended to legitimize its power. Democrats were well aware of the support the churches could give in this regard and actively sought it.

It would not have been difficult to predict this kind of reaction to the Populist challenge. One could let matters rest there had the churches not had the potentiality for a far more complex response to the general crisis of society in North Carolina. The problem becomes partly a matter of distinguishing between the conservative role of religious institutions and the otherworldly emphasis of certain kinds of piety, on the one hand, and, on the other, the radical

---

A Study in the Origins of Radical Politics (Cambridge, Mass., 1965). On the role of religion among the dispossessed, see, for example, Vincent Harding, "Religion and Resistance among Antebellum Negroes, 1800-1860," in *The Making of Black America: Essays in Negro Life and History,* eds. August Meier and Elliot Rudwick, 2 vols. (New York, 1969), 1: 179-97; and Herbert G. Gutman, "Protestantism and the American Labor Movement: The Christian Spirit in the Gilded Age," *American Historical Review* 72 (1966): 74-101.

interpretation that can be given to Christian ethical principles and the collective solidarity that religious enthusiasm can provide. The Populists, despite their criticism of the churches, were not anti-religious. Quite the contrary. Populism drew heavily on the same evangelical fervor that was the strength of the great denominations. Its democratic and egalitarian appeals struck some responsive chords within the churches. Whether or not they actively supported the People's Party, some ministers took up the cause of popular grievances.

Another group in the churches, central to this study, is crucial to an understanding of the process by which the New Order succeeded in establishing its hegemony in North Carolina. These churchmen, notably the Methodist John Carlisle Kilgo and the Baptist Josiah William Bailey, sympathized neither with populistic notions nor with the kind of passive support the churches had usually given to traditional values. A number of southern churchmen had already begun to identify themselves with the values and goals of the New South, but in the 1890s, at least in North Carolina, they acquired a heightened sense of purpose. Bailey and Kilgo explicitly rejected the doctrine limiting the church to spiritual matters and played an active role in the political struggles of the period. They appeared to recognize that the crisis of society was inescapably a crisis for the churches. In part their reaction—and that of many churchmen—was a protective one, designed to preserve the "influence" of the churches and the viability of their institutions. Hence they embarked upon a campaign to reduce the state's role in higher education in favor of the denominational colleges.

But Bailey and Kilgo had a broader vision that went beyond any desire merely to protect the churches. From their point of view, the future promised either continued instability or a realization of the New South dream. They pursued the latter possibility as the basis for a new consensus in which the churches could exert a renewed authority. Bailey and Kilgo were proposing an important ideological shift for the churches: the severing of certain ties to preindustrial southern society and the securing of others to the "progressive" capitalism of the New South. Bailey and Kilgo found important allies among businessmen who recognized the role the churches could play in securing the hegemony of the New Order. Yet the road ahead was by no means smooth. The Protestant evangelists of progress had to confront those in the denominations and

political forces in the state at large who saw an accommodation between the churches and New South capitalism as a threat to religion or their own vision of the good society or both. To the extent
that these evangelists succeeded in overcoming opposition and in
reconciling the churches, the traditional guardians of virtue and
morality, to their vision, they helped secure the future for the
New Order.

I

The Old-fashioned Gospel

THE VARIOUS IDEOLOGICAL CURRENTS that flowed through North Carolina Protestantism during the 1890s sprang from a traditional piety that in most respects was intensely conservative. Few doubted the hold that evangelical Protestantism had upon great numbers of people. Edwin A. Alderman, president of the University of North Carolina, described the state as "essentially religious, God-fearing, orthodox and Protestant." "There is no community in America," he observed in 1896, "where any form of unbelief receives less adherence, or where the clergy and the church are more influential."[1] Clerical sanctions against breaking the Sabbath were strong enough for many years to affect even the rural economy; rarely did an impious farmer challenge the prejudices of his community by cutting tobacco on Sunday.[2] From a statistical standpoint North Carolina at the turn of the century was the most Protestant state in the most Protestant section of the United States. Almost 92 percent of those southerners who claimed membership in a religious body were Protestants. In North Carolina the corresponding figure exceeded 99 percent.[3] White North Carolina Protestants, like those in the South as a whole, divided into numerous denominations, but the bulk of white church membership, 74 percent in 1906, was in three bodies: the churches associated with the Southern Baptist Convention; the Methodist Episcopal Church, South; and the Presbyterian Church in the United States. The first of these organizations contained 38 percent of the state's white Christians; the second, 28 percent; and the third, 8 percent. The

[1]Alderman, *A Brief History of North Carolina* (Boston and London, 1896), p. 45.

[2]Nannie May Tilley, *The Bright-Tobacco Industry, 1860-1929* (Chapel Hill, 1948), 59. On the influence of religion in rural North Carolina, see also Henry McGilbert Wagstaff, "A Footnote to Social History," *North Carolina Historical Review* 23 (1946): 32-46.

[3]United States Bureau of the Census, *Religious Bodies: 1906*, 2 vols. (Washington, D.C., 1910), 1: 46.

Protestant Episcopal Church, whose communicants probably carried a somewhat disproportionately large share of influence in certain communities, accounted for about 2.5 percent of North Carolina's white Protestants.[4]

In spite of theological and organizational differences, most southern denominations shared a common ethos. Refined theological disputations, apart from arguments over such things as the proper form of baptism, were not often of overriding importance except to a few professors in denominational colleges and some editors of the religious press. The conversion experience, the individual's relationship to God, personal morality, and fellowship within the church and community were what mattered most to the faithful. Their religion was fundamentalist in the sense that it consisted of an accepted body of truth—not because it necessarily embodied a set of rigidly defined "fundamental" propositions. The fundamentalist crusade was largely a twentieth-century phenomenon which reflected the partial disintegration of the old faith.[5]

In the 1890s North Carolinians, for the most part, adhered to a "primitive faith"[6] which had not really faced the implications of modern science and biblical scholarship. The evolution controversy, for example, would come later, in the 1920s. At the turn of the century William Louis Poteat taught Darwinian theory at the Baptists' Wake Forest College in North Carolina with relative impunity.[7] The editor of the *North Carolina Christian Advocate* warned preachers not to pronounce any scientific theory contrary to the Bible and pointed out that the "cosmic forces set in motion by Him only call for superior admiration and reverence by holding on and evolving with tireless energy through inconceivable eons His gracious designs."[8] Most people felt too secure in their religion, or too complacent, for intellectual abstractions and scientific

[4]These percentages were derived from data in ibid., pp. 341-44.

[5]This discussion is based on wide reading mostly in denominational newspapers. A good recent analysis of southern Protestantism is Samuel S. Hill, Jr., *Southern Churches in Crisis* (New York, 1967), especially chap. 2, "The Southern Accent in Religion," pp. 20-39. See also Kenneth K. Bailey, *Southern White Protestantism in the Twentieth Century* (New York, 1964).

[6]This phrase is from Francis Butler Simkins, "The Newer Religiousness," *Georgia Review* 4 (1950): 79.

[7]Josiah W. Bailey to Walter Hines Page, July 30, 1902, Page Papers, Houghton Library, Harvard University. See also Raleigh *News and Observer*, June 15, 1894.

[8]*North Carolina Christian Advocate*, Aug. 28, June 18, 1895.

theories to have much of a disruptive effect. It was difficult for
dogmatic assertions, either orthodox or liberal, to intrude upon a
faith that was heartfelt and intensely personal, or merely taken for
granted.

Protestantism's impact on southern culture has become a target
of criticism for those who have seen it as both a symptom and a
cause of intellectual, economic, and social decay. In 1880 David
Swing, a prominent liberal Presbyterian from Chicago, accused
southern preachers of betraying "the utmost reluctance to a faithful building up of this world in all its temporal interests." Three
decades later, H. Paul Douglass described the southern church as
"the least adaptive of the reconstructive factors of its section."[9]
Most historians and recent commentators on the South, while
acknowledging the high degree of influence exercised by the clergy
in their communities, have described southern Protestantism as
individualistic, pietistic, concerned primarily with sin, grace, judgment, and personal morality but only rarely with social ethics.[10]
"The way to appeal to the Southerner is through his religion," explained Professor John Spencer Bassett of North Carolina's Trinity
College in 1898. "The way to work reform is through the church,
but it will take a broad churchman to do it." It was Bassett's impression that most churchmen were far too narrow.[11]

Bassett was one of a number of individuals who shared the New
South ideal of progressive capitalist development. They wanted
more education, more industry, and further integration into the
mainstream of national life. But the last decade of the nineteenth
century was a depressing time for these men. They believed that
the old political elite was too strongly attached to a backward

[9]Swing, "The Failure of the Southern Pulpit," *North American Review* 130 (1880):
256-57; Douglass, *Christian Reconstruction in the South* (Boston, 1909), p. 58.

[10]For a sample of this point of view, see Hodding Carter, *Southern Legacy* Baton
Rouge, La., 1950), pp. 28-30; Virginius Dabney, *Liberalism in the South* (Chapel Hill,
1932), p. 287; Hill, passim; Benjamin Burks Kendrick and Alex Matthews Arnett, *The
South Looks at Its Past* (Chapel Hill, 1935), pp. 173-74; Howard Odum, *The Way of the
South: Toward the Regional Balance of America* (New York, 1947), pp. 170-71; George
B. Tindall, *The Emergence of the New South 1913-1945* (Baton Rouge, La., 1967), pp.
196-200; and C. Vann Woodward, *Origins of the New South* (Baton Rouge, La., 1951),
pp. 169-74, 448-53.

[11]Bassett to Herbert Baxter Adams, Dec. 16, 1898, *Historical Scholarship in the
United States, 1876-1901: As Revealed in the Correspondence of Herbert B. Adams*, ed.
W. Stull Holt (Baltimore, 1938), p. 262.

agrarian order and not possessed of the vision to provide the leadership necessary to promote progress. Bassett complained in 1896 that "it is narrow and uninspiring to live in this State just now."[12] The critics shared the conviction of the historian Stephen B. Weeks that unless the common man was educated, he would remain a "hewer of wood and drawer of water." They believed that North Carolina had to experience sweeping cultural and intellectual changes before real progress could be made. But imminent change seemed unlikely. Robert Watson Winston recalled that after Reconstruction, North Carolina was "sensitive, self-satisfied, and living in the past." For this state of affairs Walter Hines Page blamed the "mummies" among North Carolina's leading men who had suppressed real intellectual development, the basis for progress. Page often excoriated what he called the "ghost" of the Confederate dead, the "ghost" of black domination, and the "ghost" of religious orthodoxy.[13]

Page was probably the most persistent of the progressive critics in attacking the deleterious influence of the churches. He had left North Carolina in the late 1880s for a career as a journalist in Boston and New York, but he continued to expend a good deal of energy examining the ills of the South and particularly those of his native state. His ideas grew partly out of almost a lifetime of religious skepticism. As a young man he had considered a career in the ministry, but, as he told his fiancée in 1880, the churches demanded too much orthodoxy for his tastes. He described his attitude as one of "reverent unbelief."[14] In a commencement address at the University of North Carolina in 1891, Page spelled out his differences with the Old Order and presented his views on traditional politics and religion in unmistakable terms. He told the graduates:

[12]Bassett to Adams, Jan. 16, 1896, ibid., p. 243. See also Edwin A. Alderman to Walter Hines Page, Aug. 8, 1896, Page Papers. For a reminiscence by one of the intellectual critics, see Edwin Mims, "A Semi-Centennial Survey of North Carolina's Intellectual Progress," *North Carolina Historical Review* 24 (1947): 235-57.

[13]Weeks to Bennehan Cameron, Jan. 2, 1899, Cameron Papers, Southern Historical Collection, University of North Carolina Library, Chapel Hill; Winston, *It's a Far Cry* (New York, 1937), p. 94; Burton J. Hendrick, *The Training of an American: The Earlier Life and Letters of Walter Hines Page* (Boston and New York, 1928), pp. 175-92; Robert D. W. Connor, "Walter Hines Page, Southern Nationalist," in *Southern Pioneers in Social Interpretation,* ed. Howard W. Odum (Chapel Hill, 1925), p. 55.

[14]Page to Willia Alice Wilson, Jan. 4, 1880, Page Papers. For Page's early career, see Hendrick.

Renounce forever all servitude to ecclesiasticism and partyism and set out to be the ruling and shaping force among the energies that stir the people and are making of the old fields a new earth, of our long-slumbering land a resounding workshop. . . .

To every mendicant tradition that asks favors of you; to every narrow ecclesiastical prejudice that shall demand tribute . . . —to them all say with kindness, but with firmness:

"Go honored, hence, go home,
Night's childless children: here your day
   is done. . . ."[15]

The churches, according to Page, had allied themselves with all the reactionary forces that made for ignorance and decay. Page's *World's Work* declared that "war, poverty, illiteracy, epidemics and tornadoes have all done less hurt to the South than (be it said with respect to all men of breadth and tolerance) the politicians and the preachers."[16]

The qualities of southern religion that characterized its place in the total culture and annoyed the progressive critics derived from a long and partly unique history. Southern evangelical Protestantism comprised a number of sectarian religious movements that took shape in an environment which maintained frontier characteristics even in older settled regions. It lacked the deep roots—despite Anglican establishment in the southern colonies—that even antebellum northern revivalism had in the churchly tradition of New England Puritanism.[17] Some southern churchmen were aware of the difference. The *North Carolina Christian Advocate* attributed Yankee ingenuity to the "Puritan influence." The Yankee's "manual skill together with mental culture," the *Advocate* observed, as it lamented the southerner's contrary qualities, "has placed his section

[15]Quoted in Kemp P. Battle, *History of the University of North Carolina*, 2 vols. (Raleigh, 1907-12), 2: 466.

[16]*World's Work* 2 (1901): 798. See also Page, *The Rebuilding of Old Commonwealths* (New York, 1902), p. 26. For points of view similar to Page's, see John F. Crowell, *Personal Recollections of Trinity College, North Carolina, 1887-1894* (Durham, 1939), p. 240; John Spencer Bassett to Herbert Baxter Adams, Nov. 15, 1898, *Historical Scholarship in the United States*, pp. 256-59.

[17]Perry Miller sees some similarities between North and South in his essay, "From Covenant to the Revival," in *The Shaping of American Religion*, ed. James Ward Smith and A. Leland Jamison (Princeton, N.J., 1961), pp. 322-68. See also Timothy L. Smith, *Revivalism and Social Reform* (New York, 1957), p. 78; Walter Brownlow Posey, *Religious Strife on the Southern Frontier* (Baton Rouge, La., 1965), passim.

in the forefront of our civilization, for it is not the ordinary, however abundant, but the extraordinary that wins in the competition." The "long continued discipline, the persistent, uncompromising demand for absolute accuracy in the smallest details," it concluded, "eventuates in the warp and woof that issues from every loom so that goods are half sold from their creation."[18]

It would be easy to overstate differences in the sections' religious traditions. The concrete conditions of southern society were perhaps more important. Most southerners did not directly feel the pressures of immigration, industrialization, and urbanization which the northern churches were encountering. Early in the twentieth century Robert H. Pitt, the editor of the Richmond *Religious Herald,* maintained that the South's rural environment was the most important factor shaping the region's religious life. "Only here and there," he wrote, "has foreign immigration made itself felt. . . . The tide of materialism while it is rising in the South has not yet overwhelmed it. The great masses of people retain the simple manners and continue to observe the religious usages of their fathers."[19] The preaching of the old-fashioned gospel and of personal morality seemed sufficient to meet the religious needs of people who sought to set themselves right with God. Conversion itself did not require anything beyond saving faith and individual rectitude.[20] The fellowship of the congregation and the emotionalism of the revival seemed to provide sufficient comfort in the face of the South's endemic poverty. Broadus Mitchell has recalled that the two themes running through his Virginia childhood were poverty and religion; the first, he said, was the occasion of the second. Revivalism in the post-bellum South could offer a release from worldly cares without acting as a spur to aggressive action in the world.[21]

Many southerners assumed that their churches were spiritual institutions alone. Both before and after the Civil War, southern churchmen persistently appealed to this doctrine of the spiritual

[18]Aug. 21, 1895.

[19]Pitt, "Denominational Accomplishment," in *History of the Social Life of the South,* ed. Samuel C. Mitchell (Richmond, 1909), pp. 434-35.

[20]On these points see the revealing discussion in Victor I. Masters, *Baptist Missions in the South: A Century of the Saving Impact of a Great Spiritual Body on Society in the Southern States* (Atlanta, 1918), pp. 13-24.

[21]Broadus Mitchell and George S. Mitchell, *The Industrial Revolution in the South* (Baltimore, 1930), pp. 272-73.

nature of the church. They asserted that the concept of social ethics contradicted true spirituality and that the church must shun anything that smacked of political and social criticism. Salvation and individual morality were the only proper provinces of clerical concern.[22] In line with their tendency to define themselves in terms antagonistic to the presumed characteristics of the Yankee, southerners regarded the belief that the church had a right to "interfere" in secular matters as the "Northern principle" which made for the most "radical difference" between northern and southern Protestantism.[23] But the churches were so closely knit into the fabric of the region's life that their very "purity" paradoxically sanctioned cultural values. Southern traditions had such strongly moral connotations that to uphold them seemed not to violate the spirituality doctrine at all. To support consensual attitudes that were taken to be a part of the divinely ordained scheme of things did not appear to involve meddling in politics. The southern "sects" thus assumed, according to Ernst Troeltsch's typology, the function of a "church" in a very real sense; that is, they became a means for "civilizing" members of society, a mechanism of hegemony.[24] The churches were effective in this regard partly by virtue of the fact that as institutions they derived so much of their strength from the vitality of popular religion. As long as popular piety could be contained within these institutions and did not seek expression in socially subversive ways, the power of religion in maintaining social stability was considerable. American denominationalism in general has often identified itself with dominant cultural values and also performed a hegemonic function.[25] But since the North was more heterogeneous socially and religiously than the South, northern churches and religious movements often found themselves caught in struggles between competing ideologies.

[22] For a critical analysis of the doctrine of the spiritual nature of the church, see Ernest Trice Thompson, *The Spirituality of the Church: A Distinctive Doctrine of the Presbyterian Church, U.S.* (Richmond, 1961). Thompson errs, however, when he states that the doctrine is peculiar to southern Presbyterians (p. 7).

[23] C. R. Vaughn, "Organic Union," *Presbyterian Quarterly* 1 (1887): 324.

[24] Troeltsch, *The Social Teachings of the Christian Churches,* 2 vols. (London and New York, 1956), 2: 461.

[25] See, for example, the discussion in Sidney Mead, *The Lively Experiment: The Shaping of Christianity in America* (New York, Evanston, and London, 1963), especially chap. 8, pp. 134-55.

Perhaps more than anything else the existence of the churches in a slave society which was defending itself against attacks from the North was responsible for the close identification of religion with hegemonic ideology in the South. Before the Civil War many church leaders in both sections of the country attempted to forestall the disruption of the great national denominations over slavery by evading the issue as much as possible and enforcing an official silence at least in the churches' national councils. Clergymen in the South rationalized their silence by employing the doctrine of the spiritual nature of the church. The biblical defense of slavery, to which southern ministers often resorted, was usually an attempt to show that slavery was not a moral evil and hence not a fit subject for the church's condemnation. They argued that slavery was a civil matter which only properly constituted political bodies could deal with. When the southern churches eventually withdrew from the national denominations over the question of slavery, they invariably justified their course by appealing to the doctrine of the spiritual nature of the church.[26] The southern Baptist Richard Fuller pointed out to a northern colleague at the time of the southern Baptist secession that Christianity operated only indirectly in the social and political spheres "through the spirit of its precepts and the character of its professors." "The object of the gospel," he insisted, "is to turn the heart from sin to holiness. . . . The revolutions it achieves in social manners and establishments, are only secondary effects; and therefore the operation of the gospel as to these is indirect and secondary." Fuller argued that scripturally slavery was not a sin and therefore the church had no business espousing either its maintenance or its abolition.[27] Nevertheless, such a position could only have supported the interests of the plantation regime, especially since it usually required the expenditure of a good deal of energy in demonstrating that slavery was not sinful and in prescribing the duties and obligations of masters and slaves.

[26]Robert G. Torbet, *A History of the Baptists* (Philadelphia, 1950), pp. 283-313; Donald G. Mathews, *Slavery and Methodism: A Chapter in American Morality* (Princeton, N.J., 1965), pp. 274-82; Thomas Cary Johnson, *History of the Southern Presbyterian Church* (New York, 1894), pp. 311-479; Robert Ellis Thompson, *History of the Presbyterian Church in the United States* (New York, 1895), p. 331.

[27]Richard Fuller and Francis Wayland, *Domestic Slavery Considered as a Scriptural Institution* (New York and Boston, 1845), pp. 207-9.

Southern churchmen not only feared the divisive consequences of the slavery issue on the national organizations of the churches; they also believed that unless they accommodated themselves to their section's attachment to the peculiar institution, they might lose whatever influence and status they possessed. When southern Methodists withdrew from the General Conference of the church in 1844, they declared "that the continued agitation on the subject of slavery and abolition in a portion of the Church . . . must produce a state of things in the South which renders a continuance of the jurisdiction of this General Conference over these [southern] Conferences inconsistent with the success of the ministry in the slaveholding States."[28] Only by "keeping aloof from the strongest forms of direct antagonism with civil authority and State laws" could the church "maintain a footing in the South proper at all."[29] Only if the church remained faithful to its spiritual task, insisted a southern Presbyterian theologian on the eve of secession, could the church hold "the position of influence which she ought to occupy. If she undertakes to meddle with the things of Caesar, she must expect to perish by the sword of Caesar."[30]

Their antebellum experience, then, helped to make the southern denominations at least the indirect supporters of dominant social, economic, and political groups—those who identified their interests with those of the South as a whole. The doctrine of the spiritual nature of the church was remarkably well-suited to the defense of a southern civilization based on slave labor. One southerner on the eve of the Civil War saw his section blending "a series of harmonious principles . . . of moral and political success." "Prominently in view stand two peculiar [institutions]: the one a pure religion; the other a perfect labor system."[31] This is not to say that the aspirations and grievances of nonslaveholding southerners did not find religious expression. Various religious controversies, ostensibly having nothing to do with social questions, such as the

[28]Quoted in Holland N. McTyeire, *A History of Methodism* (Nashville, 1884), p. 636.

[29]*History of the Organization of the Methodist Episcopal Church, South* (Nashville, 1845), p. vii.

[30]*The Collected Writings of James Henley Thornwell*, ed. John B. Adger, 2 vols. (Richmond, 1871), 2: 44.

[31]William Gregg, quoted in Eugene D. Genovese, *The Political Economy of Slavery: Studies in the Economy and Society of the Slave South* (New York, 1965), p. 200.

antimission agitation, "exhibited deep-seated class antagonisms within the South itself."[32] Nevertheless, the denominations remained wedded to the status quo, and whatever discontent there was generally expressed itself in socially innocuous ways.

The apparent overthrow of the planter regime and the experience of Reconstruction seemed to reinforce the synthesis of secular and religious values that had developed earlier. The abolition of slavery came from outside, by force; and the groups in the South that favored the policies of Radical Reconstruction depended ultimately upon northern support. The internal crisis in the South was not grave enough to shake the attachment of southern Protestantism to the traditional virtues. In any case, a Reconstruction mythology developed quickly enough to smother whatever discontent existed. Moreover, the church lacked the power to act in any meaningful way. When a southern Baptist later recalled the terror of the Ku Klux Klan, he admitted that the "preacher[s] had no heart to rebuke them and were powerless to stop them if they had had."[33] The clergy retreated to the safety of the doctrine of the spiritual nature of the church, which once again served the South's cause. The doctrine proved useful in attacking the perversity and radicalism of northern Protestantism and by extension the whole Reconstruction regime. Southern preachers shored up their defenses against a tide of sundry excesses that had engulfed the northern churches. The Reverend J. L. M. Curry preached in 1867:

Prior to the late war it has been our boast that the "isms" were not indigenous to Southern soil.... In another section preachers and politicians seem to have formed an alliance. . . . With us faith in the Christian God was well-nigh universal. . . . Atheists and infidels did not fill Southern pulpits to discourse of modern humanity and progress and development. . . . Religion was considered most pure when farthest removed from governmental interference and entangling alliances with politics. No scriptural ch[urch] can be allied with the State.[34]

[32]Bertram Wyatt-Brown, "The Antimission Movement in the Jacksonian South: A Study in Regional Folk Culture," *Journal of Southern History* 36 (1970): 502.

[33]Masters, pp. 147-48. On the Confederate churches and their reaction to the Yankee invasion, see James W. Silver, *Confederate Morale and Church Propaganda* (Tuscaloosa, Ala., 1957).

[34]Curry, "Claims of the Hour on Young Men," ms address (1867) in the Curry Papers, Manuscript Division, Library of Congress. For similar views, see Robert Louis Dabney, *A Defense of Virginia, (and through Her, of the South,) in Recent and Pending Contests*

The image of the heroic, "scriptural" southern preacher soon became deeply embedded in the Reconstruction legend, thereby revealing the contradiction evident in Curry's description of a "spiritual" and nonpolitical church hostile to socially and politically subversive doctrines.[35]

After Reconstruction the churches continued to provide a powerful bulwark for the status quo. Even for the critical decade of the 1890s and the years following, the evidence of denominational conservatism and complacency appeared so overwhelming as to bear out the worst fears of the progressive critics. Theological liberalism and the social gospel, although not unknown, were rare growths for which southern soil provided scant nourishment. One study of more than 250 liberal and conservative Protestant ministers between 1875 and 1915 has found that "conservatives were three times as likely as liberals to come from the South."[36] The Nashville *Christian Advocate* attributed the fortunate absence in the South of communists, socialists, and "beer-garden roughs" to the "conservative influence of Christian truth." It warned preachers to exercise "prudence, tact, conciliation" and to carry their message to all classes but to offend none. Unlike their credulous northern brethren, southerners rested secure in the knowledge that "Christ and his gospel" provided the surest defense against "the various isms of the day," according to the *Wesleyan Christian Advocate*. The *Baptist Argus* rejoiced that the South—"the most distinctly religious country in the world"—was "largely free from infidelity, agnosticism, fanaticism and other destructive beliefs."[37]

In 1903 the Raleigh *News and Observer* defended traditional spiritual religion in the terms the progressive critics found so disturbing: "The business of the preacher is primarily to call men to repentance. . . . The worldly minded man, the man who gives little

---

against the Sectional Party (New York, 1867); Simon P. Richardson, *Lights and Shadows of Itinerant Life: An Autobiography* (Nashville and Dallas, 1901), pp. 234-35.

[35]See, for example, the character of Rev. John Durham in Thomas Dixon, *The Leopard's Spots: A Romance of the White Man's Burden* (New York, 1902).

[36]William R. Hutchison, "Cultural Strain and Protestant Liberalism," *American Historical Review* 76 (1971): 394, 408-9. But for evidence of religious liberalism, see John Lee Eighmy, "Religious Liberalism in the South during the Progressive Era," *Church History* 38 (1969): 359-72.

[37]Nashville *Christian Advocate*, Apr. 3, 1880, Nov. 18, 1882; *Wesleyan Christian Advocate* (Atlanta), Jan. 8, 1896; *Baptist Argus* (Louisville), Jan. 3, 1907.

thought to the call of the gospel upon him, will never be reached by the preacher who talks politics, ethics, and civil government to him. The preacher who will call that man to righteousness must be tremendously in earnest and must rely on nothing but the old-fashioned preaching of the old-fashioned gospel."[38] Despite the overwhelming evidence of the churches' social conservatism, this editorial was not a description of the practice of the day but an attack on influential churchmen who had a different conception of their task. When Josephus Daniels, the *News and Observer*'s editor, published these words, he was acutely aware that the "old-fashioned gospel" had emerged amidst the social discontent and ideological conflict of the 1890s as a very real issue in North Carolina.

[38]Dec. 6, 1903.

II

The War on the University

IT WAS IRONIC that the Raleigh *News and Observer,* a Democratic newspaper, should have had to warn preachers not to stray from the path of spirituality. Since Reconstruction, Democrats had identified their party with all that was most sacred in southern tradition, including a uniquely pure religion that, unlike the Yankee variety, did not meddle in politics. In fact, the relationship between the churches and the Democracy proved less than harmonious during the 1890s. During that decade churchmen did become involved in politics in ways that some Democrats found discomforting. The issue that first drew churchmen into the political arena ostensibly had little to do with the larger struggle for power between Democrats, Populists, and Republicans. It concerned the role of the state in higher education, specifically the amount of public financial support that the state university should receive.

Many churchmen had been convinced for a long time that the University of North Carolina was unfairly drawing students away from their own struggling denominational colleges. Although they had raised the question publicly from time to time, it remained relatively innocuous politically. But by the early 1890s things had changed, and the weakened position of the Democratic party allowed the leaders of one denomination, the Baptists, to turn state aid to higher education into a major political issue. In 1894 North Carolina voters had to choose a new state legislature and a number of state officials. The incumbent Democrats had every reason to be apprehensive as they faced a united opposition, or fusion, of Republicans and Populists. The Democrats certainly did not want Baptists to take an independent political stance and muddy the political waters even more. If the Baptist offensive had little in common with that of the Populists, it did reveal some degree of discontent with the position of the churches in the Old Order. While churchmen rarely saw any serious contradiction between their own interests and those of dominant social groups, they were concerned about the welfare and, within their proper sphere, the authority of their institutions. What thus began as a kind of self-defensive political activism on the part of denominational leaders provided much of the impetus behind a reappraisal, by churchmen, politicians, and others, of the churches' role in society.

The University of North Carolina at Chapel Hill coexisted uneasily with the state's denominational colleges after its reopening in 1875. All institutions of higher learning, not to mention elementary and secondary schools, suffered from the state's general poverty and engaged in keen competition for the patronage of the few North Carolinians who could afford to provide their sons with a higher education. Since 1881 the university had depended upon a regular appropriation from the legislature, amounting by 1884 to $20,000 a year. This sum did not seem inconsiderable at the time, considering the poverty of the state and the tight budgets on which the colleges operated. Tuition payments from a handful of students or a few hundred dollars in gifts might mean the difference between keeping the doors of a school open or closing them. Moreover, a legislative appropriation—whatever its size—set a precedent. Denominational leaders believed that state aid threatened to injure the competitive standing of privately endowed colleges.[1]

The agricultural depression that began in the 1880s heightened the churches' sense of desperation. Wake Forest, the Baptist college, counted 233 students in 1890-91, but by the winter of 1892 this number had dropped to 185.[2] At the same time enrollment in the university increased from 198 in 1891 to 316 in 1893 and 389 in 1894. For this discrepancy the denominational colleges blamed university President George Tayloe Winston's policy of offering numerous scholarships, which, they assumed, appropriations from the legislature made possible. Winston told the legislature in 1893 that 126 students "who could not otherwise be educated" received free tuition.[3] Baptists accused the university of "alluring many

---

[1]For a general discussion of the conflict during this period, see Luther L. Gobbel, *Church-State Relationships in Education in North Carolina since 1776* (Durham, 1938), pp. 74-171.

[2]Ibid., pp. 132-33.

[3]George Washington Paschal, *History of Wake Forest College,* 3 vols. (Wake Forest, 1935-43), 2: 293-94.

boys from Baptist homes and preventing the numerical growth which justly belongs to the Baptist college."[4] Meanwhile, the state had established two additional institutions of higher learning with which the sectarian colleges had to compete, the Agricultural and Mechanical College at Raleigh in 1887 and the State Normal and Industrial College for Women at Greensboro in 1891.[5]

For a variety of reasons the Baptists assumed the leadership of the state aid fight in 1894. The Methodists would join them two years later, for they shared many of the Baptist grievances against the university. They did not play an active role in 1894 largely because President John Franklin Crowell of the Methodists' Trinity College refused to become involved in the fight. His attitude perhaps indicated that the Baptists' reasons for opposing state aid were not entirely economic, for Trinity's financial circumstances were scarcely better than Wake Forest's.[6] Although Crowell, a northerner and a graduate of Yale, later recalled that "the competition for students was at the bottom of the controversial relations," he significantly pointed out that "the Methodist attitude and also the Presbyterian was as a rule far more tolerant and modern toward the aspirations of the University to expand its program by larger State appropriations."[7] As far as the Methodists were concerned, however, Crowell was taking a risk in speaking for anyone but himself.

The only nearly consistent exceptions among the denominations were the Presbyterians and Episcopalians. The latter were numerically very weak in North Carolina and did not maintain a college there. President John B. Shearer of Davidson, the Presbyterian college, only briefly joined the antagonists of appropriations in 1893 when he proposed the complete restructuring of North Carolina's system of higher education by limiting the university to graduate

[4]Charles B. Williams, *A History of the Baptists in North Carolina* (Raleigh, 1901), p. 175.

[5]Gobbel, p. 133.

[6]On Trinity's financial condition and Crowell's administration, see Earl W. Porter, *Trinity and Duke, 1892-1894: Foundations of Duke University* (Durham, 1964), pp. 1-53.

[7]Crowell to William K. Boyd, Feb. 4, 1922, Boyd Papers, Duke University Archives. See also Crowell, "Higher Education in State Constitutions," *Regents Bulletin*, no. 22 (Albany, N.Y., 1893), pp. 334-43.

and professional training.[8] Edwin A. Alderman, president of the university from 1895 to 1900, was a Presbyterian and maintained excellent relations with the leading men of that denomination. Alexander J. McKelway, the editor of the *Presbyterian Standard,* praised Alderman for being a "loyal Presbyterian" and denounced the "senseless attacks" on the university.[9] Most Presbyterians had traditionally been friendly to the university and during the 1890s generally supported state aid.[10]

The attitude of the Presbyterians and Episcopalians suggested one of the reasons behind the Baptist and, to a lesser extent, Methodist fear of the university's competition. For years the two largest denominations had complained of an inordinate amount of Presbyterian and Episcopalian influence at Chapel Hill. They pointed out that every president of the university, as well as almost all members of the faculty, had been Presbyterians or Episcopalians.[11] Methodists and Baptists were reluctant to see the university reopen in 1875 and only gave their grudging support after the trustees selected a faculty of seven which included a Methodist preacher and an associate editor of the state Baptist newspaper.[12] Cornelia Phillips Spencer, an old friend of the university and a prominent Presbyterian laywoman, rather optimistically hoped that the churches' "grudge against the uni[versity], will be appeased."[13] As another gesture of conciliation the administration at Chapel Hill during the 1880s regularly invited guest preachers from all denominations to deliver Sunday evening sermons in Gerrard Hall and awarded numerous honorary degrees to prominent churchmen, including

---

[8]Gobbel, pp. 137-38; Kemp P. Battle, *History of the University of North Carolina,* 2 vols. (Raleigh, 1907-12), 2: 479-80; Josephus Daniels, *Tar Heel Editor* (Chapel Hill, 1939), p. 464; Charles Lee Raper, *The Church and Private Schools of North Carolina: A Historical Study* (Greensboro, 1898), pp. 162-63; J. Rumple, "John Bunyan Shearer, in *Biographical History of North Carolina,* ed. Samuel A. Ashe, 8 vols. (Greensboro, 1905-17), 8: 453.

[9]McKelway to Alderman, Aug. 1897, University of North Carolina Papers, University of North Carolina Archives. See also Jonas Barclay to Alderman, July 20, 1897, ibid.

[10]Henry McGilbert Wagstaff, *Impressions of Men and Movements at the University of North Carolina* (Chapel Hill, 1950), p. 41.

[11]Nora C. Chaffin, *Trinity College, 1839-1892: Beginnings of Duke University* (Durham, 1950), p. 205; Gobbel, p. 70; Paschal, 2: 70; Wagstaff, p. 41.

[12]Battle, 2: 81; Robert W. Winston, *It's a Far Cry* (New York, 1937), pp. 74-75.

[13]Spencer to Mrs. D. L. Swain, Sept. 30, 1876, *Selected Papers of Cornelia Phillips Spencer,* ed. Louis R. Wilson (Chapel Hill, 1953), p. 693.

the presidents of Davidson, Trinity, and Wake Forest. According to the Raleigh *State Chronicle,* the degrees were "judiciously placed."[14]

In the long run the university's attempt at appeasement failed. Not only did Presbyterians and Episcopalians dominate the university's administration and faculty, but the young men of those denominations seemed to benefit disproportionately from the existence of the institution. The Presbyterians, who had their own college in North Carolina, accounted for only 8 percent of the state's white church members and the Episcopalians, a mere 2.5 percent. Yet of those students who attended the university between 1877 and 1890 and who indicated their religious affiliation, 30 percent were Presbyterian and 22 percent were Episcopalian.[15] As graduates of the university they benefited from its considerable prestige in the state, and constituted a significant proportion of the educated elite.

The hegemony of the Old Order, which identified itself strongly with the university, depended upon a community of interest and feeling between the ruling class and at least the leaders of the great evangelical churches. But denominational resentment of the university invited only abuse and contempt. One Methodist spoke fretfully of "aristocratic Presbyterians" while another worried about the "prevailing prejudices" of Episcopalians toward his church.[16] As early as 1881 Cornelia Spencer defended the university as an antidote to sectarian, that is, Baptist and Methodist, prejudice: "If the sects want to breed up a race of sectarians, ready to cut each other's throats—all the more let there be one spot in the State where they shall be compelled to meet each other on equal ground—compelled to respect each other's rights, & be taught a breadth & liberality & a degree of common sense which a State

[14]Gobbel, pp. 128-29.

[15]These figures were derived from the *Alumni History of the University of North Carolina* (Durham, 1924). Of all of the entries for this period, 266 indicated religious affiliation and 208 did not. Methodists accounted for 29 percent of the students, but Baptist students amounted to a mere 12 percent of the total. For data on church membership in the state see pp. 8-9 above.

[16]Robert L. Flowers to John C. Kilgo, Aug 16, 1897, and J. E. White to Kilgo, Dec. 1900, Trinity College Papers, Duke Univ. Archives.

education alone can give."[17] Another friend of the university characterized the campaign against state aid as "a fight for selfishness and self-aggrandizement." "Bigotry and intolerance and denominational foolery," he insisted, "are at the bottom of it all."[18] The Episcopalian former president of the university wrote in concern to the Presbyterian president of the normal college for women: "Your Presbyterian friends should understand that the object of [the Baptists] is to get control of N.C. as the Baptists have of Ga. They will have it if they can abolish higher education by the state."[19] A Methodist, on the other hand, complained of expressions like "narrow ecclesiastics . . . that have been used by bigoted state school men within recent months."[20] The state Baptist newspaper, the *Biblical Recorder,* noted that "education is not a secular matter, but is a part of the church's mission."[21] How could the largest church, the most popular of the churches, fulfill that mission if the state's leaders, supported by two of the smallest churches, continued to frustrate it?

This sense of frustration led the Baptists to take advantage of the keen political competition between the Democrats and Populist-Republican fusionists. They injected the state aid issue into the campaign of 1894 and tried to convince the electorate to support only those candidates, regardless of party, who sympathized with the denominational cause. The Baptists labored throughout the year in anticipation of the election in November and the convening of the new legislature in January. President Charles Elisha Taylor of Wake Forest College furnished the ideological justification for the Baptist campaign in a skillfully written series of articles for the *Biblical Recorder* which appeared during April and May. Since Baptist leaders wanted Taylor's arguments to influence as many people as possible, they reprinted his articles in a forty-eight-page pamphlet entitled *How Far Should a State Undertake*

[17]Spencer to Miss Patterson, Feb. 22, 1881, Samuel Finley Patterson Papers, Duke University Library.

[18]Charles L. Coon to George T. Winston, July 17, 1894, UNC Papers.

[19]Kemp P. Battle to Charles D. McIver, Apr. 12, 1894, McIver Papers, Library of the University of North Carolina at Greensboro. See also Birdie Bell to McIver, Oct. 14, 1894, ibid.

[20]J. A. Baldwin to Walter Hines Page, May 21, 1897, Page Papers, Houghton Lib., Harvard Univ.

[21]Dec. 12, 1894.

to Educate? or, A Plea for the Voluntary System in Higher Education and distributed 25,000 copies.[22] The pamphlet lacked the polemical edge of the speeches and writings of other clerical spokesmen, but it soon became the standard authority for the opponents of appropriations. Even a supporter of the university admitted that Taylor's views were "temperate and able."[23]

Taylor stated frankly that unless the people of North Carolina repudiated the state's claims in the realm of higher education, "very many private institutions must die." But on the whole he argued less from a standpoint of denominational self-interest than from abstract principle and political expediency. Supporters of state aid, he insisted, could defend their position only by appealing to a paternalistic theory of government. Taylor believed that paternalism was an undesirable legacy of the old notion of rule by divine right and had no place in a republican society. He devised a syllogism to show that it was unjust for the legislature to support the university. First he assumed that "true" higher education had to contain religious elements. But the state's fundamental law prohibited it from aiding the establishment of religion. Hence, Taylor reasoned, the state could not provide the proper kind of higher education without violating the principle of separation of church and state.[24]

Taylor anticipated a line of argument that might be used against the Baptists by denying that denominational opposition to state aid to the university implied any hostility to public support of the common schools. On the contrary, he tried to show that the miserable condition of North Carolina's public schools made appropriations for higher education inexpedient. North Carolina was a poor state which ought to use its limited resources where they would do the most good; the state simply could not afford a university. Taylor insisted that his advocacy of public elementary education was in no way inconsistent with his opposition to university appropriations. Common schools, unlike universities, were necessary for the preservation of the state. A popular representative government

[22]*Minutes of the Annual Meeting of the Baptist State Convention of North Carolina . . . 1895*, p. 58. Taylor's pamphlet was published in Raleigh in 1894.

[23]Josephus Daniels, *Editor in Politics* (Chapel Hill, 1941), p. 103.

[24]Pp. 16, 9, 29.

required that its citizens obtain the rudiments of good citizenship which only education could provide.[25]

The Reverend Christopher Columbus Durham, the corresponding secretary of the North Carolina Baptist convention, assumed the task of disseminating the arguments against appropriations throughout the state. Unlike Taylor, who was an even-tempered man and "shrank from a tussle on the hustings," Durham was eager for a good fight.[26] Durham had been a severe critic of the university at least since the early 1880s.[27] He was a member of the committee appointed by the 1893 Baptist convention to memorialize the next legislature "on the friction and competition between the State schools and the denominational schools."[28] Durham canvassed the state from the mountains to the sea and carried his message to Baptist congregations and most of the church's local associations. He tried to place Taylor's pamphlet within reach of every Baptist home.[29] The Baptist press carried glowing reports of Durham's progress. When he spoke at the associations during September and October, large crowds reportedly gathered to hear him. Excitement ran high. An agent of the *Biblical Recorder* claimed that west of Greensboro 90 percent of the people were opposed to the state's educational policy. "It looks here," the agent reported from Wilkesboro, "as it does in other places where I have been, that the people are all one way on this subject."[30] A supporter of state aid confided to President Charles D. McIver of the normal college that an address by Durham in Rutherfordton "won many over on his side who were friends of the State schools before."[31] Durham seemed to be waging a holy war.

But Durham's intransigent self-righteousness also aroused bitter antagonism. According to Josephus Daniels, the Baptist secretary had not "the least shadow of humor" and in his fight against the

[25] Pp. 20-21.

[26] Paschal, 2: 294, n. 5. See also Daniels, *Editor in Politics*, p. 103.

[27] Gobbel, p. 83.

[28] *Minutes of the Annual Meeting of the Baptist State Convention of North Carolina . . . 1893*, p. 56.

[29] Paschal, 2: 303; Daniels, *Editor in Politics*, p. 103; Williams, p. 176.

[30] *Biblical Recorder*, Sept. 12, Sept. 5, 1894. See also Sept. 19, 1894.

[31] Birdie Bell to McIver, Oct. 14, 1894, McIver Papers.

university "asked no quarter and gave none."[32] Supporters of the university despised the intrepid Baptist and accused him of all manner of unscrupulousness. Mrs. Spencer charged him with "bigotry and ignorance and hatred and falsehood and stupidity and envy and selfishness and apathy and jealousy and folly and all uncharitableness."[33] Even Durham's friends, who were enthusiastic about his abilities, occasionally felt constrained to excuse the extravagant qualities of his character.[34] A year and a half after Durham's premature death in 1895 one of his closest associates privately admitted that the Baptist secretary had "lost his head" during the state aid fight.[35] President Winston was probably right when he remarked that Durham had in him the "elements of the martyr."[36]

While Durham was rallying the Baptists across the state, the *Biblical Recorder* reminded the brethren of their duty to register their convictions with their ballots in the November election. The official editor of the *Recorder,* the Reverend C. T. Bailey, was incapacitated by illness, but his son, Josiah William, though only in his twenties, was no less capable of running an effective newspaper. He officially became editor of the *Recorder* upon his father's death in July 1895 and held this position until 1907 although he never entered the ministry. He then followed the allurements of politics, which led to a seat in the United States Senate in 1930.[37] The younger Bailey wanted state aid to be "the issue" in the political campaign and looked forward to a "ground-swelling of public opinion" that would carry the day for the Baptists. He told his readers, "We want the man—without regard to party—in whom temperance and educational principles are thoroughly mixed."[38]

[32]*Editor in Politics,* p. 102.

[33]Cornelia Spencer to George T. Winston, Mar. 26, 1895, UNC Papers. See also William Cain (a professor at the university) to his sister, Dec. 2, 1894, John Steele Henderson Papers, Southern Hist. Coll., UNC Lib.; George T. Winston to Augustus W. Graham, Apr. 23, 1894, Graham Papers, ibid.

[34]*Biblical Recorder,* Nov. 20, 1891.

[35]Josiah W. Bailey to John C. Kilgo, June 14, 1897, Trinity College Papers.

[36]*Biblical Recorder,* Nov. 28, 1894.

[37]Bailey agonized at times over whether he should enter the ministry (Bailey to John C. Kilgo, [Dec. 1901], and June 26, 1902, Trinity College Papers). For an overview of Bailey's career, see John Robert Moore, *Senator Josiah William Bailey of North Carolina: A Political Biography* (Durham, 1968).

[38]*Biblical Recorder,* July 4, 1894. See also Aug. 8, 1894.

Bailey hoped that Baptists would not "hold their principles in abeyance for partisan reasons," for the church was fighting the Lord's battle. The state aid issue transcended normal political considerations. "Each man," he observed, "is asked to vote the dictates of his conscience, each Christian must determine—must say by his vote—'who is on the Lord's side!' "[39] With this assertion Bailey committed the Baptists to political activism. In his terms the battle was joined, not between advocates of two different educational principles, but between the minions of Satan and the children of God. The doctrine of the spiritual nature of the church could hardly be a deterrent to political action when so much was at stake.

The Baptist drive was disconcerting not only to officials of the university but to leaders of the Democratic party as well. Both believed that at least an informal alliance existed between the preachers and the fusionists. The Democratic party had closely identified itself with the interests of the university, and the party's retention of power helped to preserve the authority of those "aristocratic" elements in the state which the Baptists and Populists—for different reasons—opposed. Durham promised the Democratic Raleigh *News and Observer* that the Baptists would tolerate "no compromise, no side-track for this question, and no cessation of aggressive agitation."[40] Such language worried the paper's editor. Daniels believed that most Baptist preachers and many laymen had fallen under Durham's influence. Tarheels were aware that in neighboring South Carolina, Benjamin R. Tillman had attacked that state's university in his insurgent campaign against the traditional Democratic elite; in fact he may have indirectly profited from the denominational opposition to state aid there.[41] The *News and Observer* warned that "to tear the State to pieces by new quarrels and jealousies over this subject [state aid] would be calamitous."[42] Moreover, unity was obviously necessary to preserve Democratic supremacy.

[39] Ibid., Oct. 24, 1894.

[40] Columbus Durham to the Raleigh *News and Observer*, Sept. 28, 1894.

[41] Daniels, *Editor in Politics*, p. 102; George T. Winston to Cornelia Phillips Spencer, Apr. 9, 1895, Spencer Papers, 1859-1905, p.c. 7, North Carolina State Archives; William J. Cooper, Jr., *The Conservative Regime: South Carolina, 1877-1890* (Baltimore, 1968), pp. 41-43, 54.

[42] July 1, 1894.

Fusion candidates campaigned for a reduction in state expenditures and accused the Democrats of using the state's institutions, including the university, for partisan advantage.[43] This attitude seemed to place the fusionists, at least by implication, on the side of the Baptists. After the overwhelming Democratic defeat at the polls in November, the Wilmington *Messenger* lamented that one of the policies of the new legislature would be the "repeal of State aid to the venerable and most useful university of North Carolina."[44] William Cain, a professor at Chapel Hill, concluded that the war on the university "helped very naturally to elect Rads.-Pops." He believed that continued Baptist agitation against the university would prevent a Democratic victory for some time, "as presumably the democrats being of a higher grade than the rad pops are more generally for us."[45] One "prominent" Democrat flatly stated that the Baptist fight caused no less than nineteen counties to swing away from his party. He considered the state aid agitation the "great disorganizer" of the campaign and attributed Populist successes to the thirty-three speeches that Durham made during the months before the election.[46]

During the campaign the Baptists had shown that they were willing to go to almost any lengths politically to achieve their ends, confirming in the minds of many Democratic leaders the old conviction that preachers should stick to their spiritual calling. In Wake County, whose seat is Raleigh, the state capital, the fusion nominee for the senate was an avowed opponent of state aid while the Democratic nominee was a supporter of appropriations. The Democrat lost.[47] In many other counties the fusionists attacked the university in order to gain the support of the Baptist clergy.[48] In Gaston County the Reverend M. P. Matheny wrote an open letter to Frank P. Hall, the Democratic candidate for the house of representatives, demanding that he should publicly take a stand on the state aid issue. When Hall refused to commit himself, Matheny sent a second

[43]Raleigh *Progressive Farmer*, Sept. 25, 1894.

[44]Quoted in the Raleigh *News and Observer*, Dec. 4, 1894.

[45]Cain to his sister, Dec. 2, 1894, Henderson Papers.

[46]Charlotte *Observer*, Dec. 1, 1894.

[47]Ibid., Nov. 20, 1894.

[48]Daniels, *Editor in Politics*, p. 102.

letter in which he threatened to endorse the fusion nominee, who happened to oppose state aid. Hall then charged that Matheny had been using his "pastoral visits for the past six months to sow his political seeds." Finally, according to Hall, Matheny's congregation demanded that the preacher "not use the church as a base of supplies while he makes war on the Democratic party." Faced with a revolt in his own flock, Matheny, again according to Hall, announced that he had no intention of putting any candidate's election in jeopardy. Even so, the *Biblical Recorder* came to Matheny's defense and charged that Hall was an "upstart candidate" who could not "conceal his ears or restrain his bray." The Democratic Charlotte *Observer* replied that the Baptist weekly was using "the language of the slums" and was "maddened out of reason" because it could not "bulldoze" Hall. But when the votes were counted, Hall lost to the fusionists' candidate.[49]

Although in Matheny's case a congregation had apparently opposed its minister's political activism, the Charlotte *Observer* had to admit after the election "that already several country churches have disciplined their pastors for voting the Democratic ticket." The paper did not say whether these congregations supported the fusionists because of the state aid issue or for other reasons, but whatever the case, those who had raised the state aid issue in the first place were to blame. "If any church court may tell the state of North Carolina what to do and what not to do in regard to higher education," the *Observer* concluded, "why may not a little country church tell its preacher how he must vote?"[50]

The Baptists had every reason to be confident when the legislature convened in January 1895. Populists and Republicans outnumbered the Democrats by more than two to one.[51] The *Biblical Recorder* jubilantly announced that a majority in both houses opposed state aid, but for good measure it warned the members to do what the people expected of them.[52] President Winston privately feared that the *Recorder* was right, telling his friend McIver, "I

[49] The Matheny-Hall episode can be followed in the Charlotte *Observer*, Oct. 9, Nov. 2, Nov. 8, 1894, and the *Biblical Recorder*, Oct. 31, 1894.

[50] Oct. 31, 1894.

[51] Helen G. Edmonds, *The Negro and Fusion Politics in North Carolina, 1894-1901* (Chapel Hill, 1951), p. 37.

[52] Jan. 16, 1895.

think the chances are decidedly against us." Nevertheless, he worked
tirelessly to stave off defeat. Winston and his chief lieutenant, Professor Alderman, employed cautious, dilatory tactics, hoping to al-
low the Baptist offensive to wear itself out. In January, Alderman
admitted to Mrs. Spencer that the university was in "grave danger"
as a result of the "political revolution" and the "denominational
crusade." "A false step, an ill-considered word, an impolitic act,"
he wrote, "and we are seriously crippled. Our policy seems to be
silence with all our guns loaded, however, ready for action."
Winston and Alderman quietly approached individual senators and
representatives. Many legislators seemed hostile to the university at
the beginning of the session, "but," Alderman reported, "a sixty
day's residence in Raleigh is a sort of an education to utterly inex-
perienced men and it will change their ideas."[53]

The Baptists accused the university of engaging in unscrupulous
lobbying in order to thwart the will of the people. Durham charged
that Winston attempted to bribe a Populist leader, S. Otho Wilson,
by offering him the use of a scholarship for political patronage. But
despite Baptist protests, the university's efforts were paying off. By
the end of January the *Recorder* was less certain of total victory. It
discounted rumors of a caucus of "dominant elements" in the legislature which agreed not to touch university appropriations. "On
the other hand," the Baptist paper admitted, "while we cannot say
what will be done, we are confident that a step will be taken for
the right."[54]

During the campaign most important fusion leaders, as opposed
to individual candidates for the legislature, had avoided committing
themselves on the state aid question, probably in order to take political advantage of the Baptist agitation without alienating university supporters. But with the election behind them, they began
either to reconsider their position or to express the convictions
which they had held in abeyance. By the end of November, J. C. L.
("Loge") Harris, a prominent Republican, predicted that the legislature would probably not withdraw appropriations.[55] Late in
January the leading Populist paper, the Raleigh *Caucasian,* finally

[53]Winston to McIver, n.d. [early in 1895], McIver Papers; Alderman to Spencer, Jan.
17, 1895, Spencer Papers. See also George T. Winston to Spencer, Mar. 1895, ibid.

[54]*Biblical Recorder,* Dec. 12, 1894, Jan. 9, Jan. 30, 1895.

[55]Charlotte *Observer,* Nov. 25, 1894.

declared for state aid, although it urged that "state institutions be carefully inspected and . . . mismanagement be exposed and corrected."[56] In February, Marion Butler, the Populist state chairman, cautiously endorsed the continuation of the $20,000 appropriation but opposed retaining the $10,000 special appropriation that the previous legislature had granted the university. Actually friends of Butler had given assurances of his support three months earlier. His Republican counterpart, A. E. Holton, asserted "with much earnestness" that the legislature would not reduce appropriations.[57]

By January university officials were certain that the leaders of all parties supported appropriations.[58] The question was whether the fusion leadership could control the rank and file in the legislature, who in many cases had opposed state aid during the campaign. Editor Daniels was confident Butler could keep dissident Populists in line, but President Winston doubted the Populist leader's "power to catch them." In December, Winston appealed to Republican Congressman Thomas Settle to use his influence with Republicans in the legislature, reminding him that the university was the only "college in the State where men may think as they please on all subjects. . . . All parties, all denominations, all sections may confidently look to the University for its leaders."[59] To supplement his personal overtures, Winston sent to the legislature in February a masterful defense of state aid in which he argued that the university was both nonpartisan and nonsectarian. In contrast to Taylor's essentially conservative arguments and the Baptists' largely religious appeal, Winston played on the Populists' class grievances by implying that it was the private colleges that were aristocratic. At the university, on the other hand, "rich and poor . . . meet within its walls on terms of perfect quality." If the state withdrew its aid, the university would have to depend on tuition charges and could no longer afford to help "the talented poor boys of the State." Meeting Taylor's argument about saving money for

[56] Jan. 31, 1895.

[57] Raleigh *News and Observer,* Feb. 10, 1895; Logan D. Howell to Charles D. McIver, Nov. 19, 1894, McIver Papers; Charlotte *Observer,* Jan. 31, 1895.

[58] Alderman to Spencer, Jan. 17, 1895, Spencer Papers.

[59] Daniels to McIver, Nov. 9, 1894, and Winston to McIver, n.d., McIver Papers; Winston to Settle, Dec. 31, 1894, Settle Papers, Southern Hist. Coll., UNC Lib. See also Winston to Settle, Feb. 8, 1895, ibid.

the public schools, Winston defended the university as "the head" of the public school system. He pointed out that if the legislature gave the university's appropriation to the common schools, as some proposed, it would lengthen their term by only a day and a half. He showed that the university educated about sixty teachers a year and in addition maintained a regular summer teaching institute.[60]

By the time the joint committee on education met in March, the university had gained considerable ground. Since regular appropriations would continue unless explicitly repealed, the committee held public hearings on a bill to discontinue all aid to the university. A few days before the committee met, a group of Populist and Republican legislators visited Chapel Hill, and the report which they prepared enthusiastically endorsed the university's administration. Only "hard times" prevented the visiting lawmakers from recommending an actual increase in appropriations.[61]

The testimony of Durham and Winston, who appeared together before the committee, provided a stirring climax to the state aid fight. On the whole, Durham made a poor showing. According to the *News and Observer* correspondent, the two men "engaged in heated debate in which personalities were freely used." Durham claimed that the university used scholarships, among other things, as bait to lure students away from the colleges. He read a circular which stated that the university provided free of charge a limited number of rooms with service; "that means," the good preacher explained, "a nigger to wait on you." Finally, Durham told the members that scholarships were often given to the sons of men who were well-to-do and had political pull, not to poor boys.[62]

In the course of the hearings Hamilton G. Ewart, a Republican representative and a backer of state aid, questioned Durham about the recent campaign in Wake County. Everyone agreed that state aid was a major issue in the Wake election. "Were not the Democrats understood to favor the appropriations and the fusionists to oppose it?" Ewart inquired. "I believe so," came the preacher's reply. Ewart then asked how Durham himself had voted. Without

[60]Winston's arguments were printed in full in the Raleigh *News and Observer*, Feb. 3, 1895.

[61]Ibid., Mar. 5, 1895.

[62]Ibid., Mar. 6, 1895.

hedging the question, Durham admitted, "The straight Democratic ticket." "Then you didn't vote as you shot?" Ewart concluded. Durham's admission that he had not no doubt made Baptist admonitions to the brethren to vote for the "right" candidate seem rather hollow. James H. Young, a black representative, concluded that "the white Baptists did just as the Democrats always did: talked one way and voted another." The committee gave the university a stunning victory when it voted thirty-eight to two against the bill to end state aid.[63]

Josephus Daniels considered the action of the committee "remarkable" since in his view many fusionists had won their seats by denouncing the extravagance of state aid. The committee's vote had exposed the opposition's attack on the university as "false and demagogical." President Winston believed that the university's victory had saved the state from Populist "Revolutionists," a revealing expression coming from a man who had recently been so busy patronizing Populist legislators.[64] In fact, the university probably had Populist and Republican leaders more than anyone else to thank for its victory. Populists like Butler and William A. Guthrie, who were university alumni, feared that their party would make a grievous error if it opposed state aid. Like many of their contemporaries they had great faith in education as an instrument of social mobility. Daniels later admitted that Butler did "yeoman service" for the university in speeches and private conversation.[65] When Guthrie hurried to Raleigh in time to testify before the education committee, he announced, "I have come to save my party from making a fool of itself."[66] After the fight was over, Daniels hoped that since all three parties had sustained the university, no one could ever use the issue to aid the Democrats' opponents again.[67] The fusionists may have taken advantage of Baptist opposition to state aid in the campaign, but their record in the legislature appeared to commit them unequivocally to appropriations for the university in the future.

[63]Ibid., Mar. 6, Mar. 8, 1895.

[64]Ibid., Mar. 15, 1895; Winston to Spencer, Apr. 9, 1895, Spencer Papers.

[65]*Editor in Politics,* p. 103. See also Joseph G. deRoulhac Hamilton, *North Carolina since 1860* (Chicago and New York, 1919), p. 251.

[66]Daniels, *Editor in Politics,* p. 107.

[67]Raleigh *News and Observer,* Mar. 15, 1895.

The Baptists, however, were not ready to concede defeat and had no intention of taking state aid out of politics. Durham declared that the brethren would enter the next political campaign in even greater force.[68] Bailey charged that university officials had used methods that had not availed when the state's educational policy was being debated before the people but succeeded only "in the lobbies and on the street corners" of the capital. The Baptist editor insisted that Winston and Alderman had enlisted the aid of certain "leading politicians with that unaccountable power over legislators." He also hinted that Durham's human "weaknesses" might have contributed to the Baptist defeat. But, Bailey warned, "before the political conventions meet again we believe there will be enough people who believe as we do in any of the parties to effect our principles."[69]

Baptist leaders seemed quite unconcerned about having alienated important elements in the Democratic party during the campaign. After the election the Democratic press castigated the Baptist leaders for meddling in political affairs. The Charlotte *Observer* accused them of disregarding the principle of separation of church and state when they made the state university a subject for discussion at their conventions and associations. The *News and Observer* reminded the Baptists that they had traditionally confined themselves "to those things that pertained to the spiritual kingdom" and urged them to return to "the faith of their fathers." "The recent campaign," the Raleigh daily continued, "has revealed a danger that threatens the Baptist people and through them the State of North Carolina"; it might also have added the Democratic party.[70] One Baptist supporter of state aid expressed the feeling of many Democrats when he referred to the *Biblical Recorder* as "the organ of the North Carolina Baptists (published, owned and controlled as a private enterprise), devoted to Bible religion, education (provided it is not higher), and general intelligence (anti-higher educational and semi-political)."[71] In return Bailey warned Daniels that Baptists would not tolerate any "idiotic, impudent, hair-brain,

[68]Charlotte *Observer*, Mar. 7, 1895.

[69]*Biblical Recorder*, Mar. 13, 1895.

[70]Charlotte *Observer*, Dec. 7, 1894; Raleigh *News and Observer*, Nov. 25, 1894.

[71]"Baptist" to the Charlotte *Observer*, Sept. 16, 1894.

brazen, cracked-voice, cuckoo-coo tomtit chirping" from his newspaper.[72]

Democrats may have been correct in assuming that the preachers' fishing in troubled political waters helped to elect fusion candidates. The Baptist church leaders certainly were not performing their traditional hegemonic role. But outside of some localities a real alliance between Baptists and Populists (not to mention Republicans) was unlikely. Durham's admission that he voted for a Democratic candidate who supported state aid reached to the heart of the Baptists' dilemma. Durham had found it impossible to make the final break with the party that was—along with the churches—a defender of consensual values. The Baptists were waging a holy war against the university, but to do so successfully they had to fight the political party that at least since Reconstruction had regarded itself as God's chosen instrument in the South. Many other Baptists probably chose the same path as Durham. A Populist newspaper in Wake County which originally backed the Baptist cause but changed its position after the election reported that a Populist candidate who opposed appropriations made a poor showing in Wake Forest precinct itself. Baptists, the paper concluded, refused to "vote as they pray."[73]

The men who organized the Populist party had glimpsed the hegemonic character of the Old Order and finally made a decisive political break. But men like Durham and Taylor never reached the conclusion that the old consensus perhaps made the mass of the members of their churches the unwitting victims of a backward and unequal society. They thought largely in terms of denominational status and self-interest and had little sense of the other social implications of their grievances. The political activism of the Baptists in 1894 and 1895 was limited in scope and intention. With the exception of Josiah Bailey, who was beginning to strike out on an independent political course,[74] there is little evidence that anyone speaking specifically as a denominational opponent of state aid challenged the ideological assumptions of the Old Order or the role

[72]*Biblical Recorder,* Nov. 28, 1894. See also ibid., Dec. 12, 1894; Raleigh *News and Observer,* Mar. 6, 1895.

[73]Quoted in Raleigh *News and Observer,* Mar. 6, 1895.

[74]Bailey's ideological and political development is discussed in chap. 5 below.

of the churches in society. As far as the Baptists were concerned, the problem was simply the negligence of the state's leaders in protecting the legitimate interests of the churches in the realm of higher education. Yet they proved themselves no mere pawns of the old elite. They were willing to speak out forcefully against the educational priorities of the Democratic party and to attack the party itself even if, as in the case of Durham, they ended up voting for Democratic candidates. And this criticism occurred at a time when the Democracy, the party that embodied all that the Old Order stood for, was fighting for its survival. The Populists seemed to be aware of the ambiguous and inconclusive nature of the Baptists' political activity. One consequence of the war on the university was a Populist indictment of the churches' social conservatism, a far cry from the Populist-Baptist alliance that many Democrats had feared during the campaign of 1894.

III

The Populist Challenge to the Churches

THE POPULISTS could easily have allowed the religious issue to rest once the legislature of 1895 had adjourned. But in June both Marion Butler and William Guthrie used the occasion of the university's commencement to berate the Baptists for their selfish and undemocratic behavior. Butler, now elected to the United States Senate, praised the university as a friend of the poor and denounced anyone "who loved denomination or sect more than he loved the liberties of the people."[1] The day before the two Populists spoke at Chapel Hill, the Raleigh *Caucasian,* which Butler owned, had charged that men of "wealth and respectability" exercised undue influence in the churches of the Old North State. The *Caucasian* asserted that most ministers did not "dare preach Christ's socialism from their pulpits . . . without giving offense to the powers that arrange their salaries." Several days earlier the *Progressive Farmer,* the official organ of the North Carolina Farmers' Alliance, claimed that the average preacher read little besides "a milk and cider religious journal (three-fourths are that kind) and his favorite daily newspaper which is a bold advocate of gold-bug plutocracy or a cowardly straddler ninety-eight times out of a hundred."[2] Throughout most of June and July the *Caucasian* printed letters from its readers who took churches and preachers severely to task on social and political grounds. "Feed the preachers on fried chicken and sweetmeats," wrote one Populist, "and go home and live on corn-bread and buttermilk yourself."[3] The Populists were beginning to understand an important aspect of social reality in North Carolina, that the churches not only had given implicit support to traditional

[1] Raleigh *News and Observer,* June 13, 1895. See also ibid., June 8, 1895; John Ammons (a Populist legislator) to the Raleigh *Progressive Farmer,* Apr. 23, 1895.

[2] Raleigh *Caucasian,* June 6, 1895; Raleigh *Progressive Farmer,* May 21, 1895.

[3] R. H. W. Barker to the Raleigh *Caucasian,* June 20, 1895. See also J. P. R. to *Caucasian,* July 4, 1895, and Charlie Eure to *Caucasian,* July 25, 1895.

hegemonic values but had already begun to adopt the vocabulary
of New South capitalism.

Except for Butler's remarks at Chapel Hill, the criticisms of the
churches in the *Caucasian* and the *Progressive Farmer* provoked
little response from either the Democratic or the denominational
press.[4] It was otherwise with an address delivered at Cary in August
by the incoming president of the state Farmers' Alliance, Dr. Cyrus
Thompson. He told the assembled farmers (almost as an aside in a
much longer speech) that the "church today stands where it has
always stood[,] on the side of human slavery."[5] This "famous
remark," as it was generally called, precipitated a bitter political-
religious controversy. The Methodist *North Carolina Christian Advocate,* which assumed that Thompson must have spoken "in the
heat of extemporaneous discourse," could not believe that the doctor had really meant what he said.[6] Thompson, however, had
meant every word. In September he sent to the *Progressive Farmer*
an elaboration of his Cary speech which was widely reprinted in
both the Populist and Democratic press. According to the *News
and Observer,* the doctor spoke "wusser and wusser."[7]

Thompson identified his critics as the "same 'gang'" that shed
"crocodile tears" when the Farmers' Alliance went into politics by
becoming a part of the Populist movement and refusing to become
"the tool of the machine Democracy in North Carolina." He
offered no apology for his speech at Cary. He had spoken, he explained, as a Christian. Although he did not wish to harm the
church, he believed that if his criticism was just, then the church
had to suffer—and deserved to suffer—the consequences. Since the
church as a human institution was no better than the men who were
a part of it, it was just as proper, he argued, to make war upon sin
within the church as outside of it. The church that consisted only
of "pious feelings, long prayers, and sanctimonious countenances"
was not genuinely Christian. The true church, Thompson declared,
had to stand "wholly on the side of human freedom." He had "no
words but of indignation and contempt" for a church that "in a
pretended consecration to God" did not confess "its un-Christly

[4] For a response to Butler, see the *Biblical Recorder,* June 19, 1895.

[5] Quoted in the Raleigh *News and Observer,* Aug. 18, 1895.

[6] Aug. 21, 1895.

[7] Sept. 17, 1895.

disregard of man's daily needs until he is pauperized and un-manned."[8]

The Democratic reaction to Thompson's arguments was hardly surprising. No one made any serious attempt to refute them. Instead the Democrats greeted Thompson's explanation, as they had his speech at Cary, with abuse and bitter condemnation. The reasons for this kind of response were obvious. In the first place, serious criticism of a cherished institution like the church was rare in the South. Second, and perhaps more important, an attack on the churches (like an attack, for example, on white supremacy) threatened to subvert the whole complex of southern attitudes, traditions, and myths that had provided a protective covering for the hegemony of the Old Order. Following the Cary speech, Daniels's *News and Observer* expressed dismay that "not even the church of Christ can escape the denunciation of a Populist orator when he is howling before an audience." When Thompson persisted in his apostasy, the Raleigh daily lamented that "this misguided man glories in his shame."[9] The Charlotte *Observer* calmly told its readers not to be surprised at what came out of a Populist mouth. Later, with less equanimity, the *Observer* hoped Thompson would "get his head slapped off."[10] From Georgia the Atlanta *Constitution,* the organ of that state's Democratic machine, neatly summed up the reaction of the old party's adherents. It classified Thompson's "reckless utterances" with those "of the nihilists, anarchists and other enemies of society who are doing so much to disturb the peace of the world."[11] The church and the Democratic party, it seemed, together preserved the good order of society which the Populists were trying to destroy.

Thompson did not deserve the harsh language which Democratic editors used against him, and at least Daniels certainly knew it. For years both men had been active laymen in the North Carolina Annual Conference of the Methodist church. They would serve together as lay delegates to the conference in 1896.[12] Dr. Thompson

[8]Thompson in the Raleigh *Progressive Farmer,* Sept. 17, 1895. See also Raleigh *Caucasian,* Sept. 19, 1895; Raleigh *News and Observer,* Sept. 17, 1895.

[9]Aug. 18, Sept. 17, 1895.

[10]Aug. 30, Sept. 24, 1895.

[11]Quoted in the Raleigh *News and Observer,* Sept. 22, 1895.

[12]Josephus Daniels, *Editor in Politics* (Chapel Hill, 1941), pp. 298-99; *Journal of the*

was a deeply religious man whose medical practice in the rural areas of Onslow County "brought him face to face with the poverty and degradation . . . then prevailing."[13] His sense of social justice made him acutely aware of the contradiction between what he regarded as the spirit of Christianity and the actual practices of most churches. "I am not condemning the 'mystical body' of the church, whose head is the risen Christ," he insisted. "I am saying nothing of the Church which shall be the Bride of the Lamb."[14] Nor was Thompson ignorant of theology and church history. Although he claimed to be only a "simple-minded piney woods philosopher," he had read the New Testament in Greek, and his articles on the church suggested more than a passing acquaintance both with the writings of Augustine, Luther, and Calvin, among others, and with some recent developments in church historiography.[15] His religious ideas, in fact, conformed less to old-fashioned Methodism than to the Christocentric liberal theology of his day and the ethics of the social gospel. Far from being the godless ogre that the Democratic press described, Thompson was a man of considerable learning and of humane temperament, strongly committed to the ideal that the church become "a manifestation of . . . divine life flowing into human history."[16]

Thompson succeeded in articulating what many other Populists probably felt instinctively. Throughout the South and West the People's Party displayed a revivalistic fervor that bore a striking resemblance to the old-time religion. Populists both affirmed the teachings of Christianity as they construed them and attacked the churches for forsaking those teachings. In embracing a kind of popular, grass-roots social gospel, they revealed almost in spite of

North Carolina Annual Conference of the Methodist Episcopal Church, South . . . 1896, p. 102.

[13] Joseph Parsons Brown, *The Commonwealth of Onslow: A History* (New Bern, 1960), p. 121.

[14] Thompson in the Raleigh *Caucasian,* Dec. 12, 1895.

[15] Brown, pp. 124-25; Raleigh *Caucasian,* Dec. 12, Dec. 19, 1895, Jan. 2, Feb. 6, 1896.

[16] Raleigh *Caucasian,* Dec. 12, 1895. See also Thompson in the Raleigh *Progressive Farmer,* Sept. 17, 1895.

themselves that the power of evangelical Protestantism could serve more than the forces of the status quo.[17]

Despite Democratic fulminations, Thompson succeeded in bringing into the open an issue that other men had hesitated to discuss publicly. "I have referred to that position of the church in the Reform movement in my family circle," one Populist told Thompson, "but never in a public way and you are the first man in all my knowledge that has yet arraigned the pulpit for its inactivity and silence on the side of the reform of the day."[18] An outpouring of Populist support for Thompson suggested that a number of North Carolinians had become skeptical of the churches' role in southern society and of the Democratic party's claim to be the sole defender of virtue and religion. An Alliance lecturer, who was also a field-worker for the North Carolina Sunday School Association, assured Thompson that his "recent famous utterance meets with favorable comment so far as I have heard except in the News and Observer and *Democratic i.e. religious* papers."[19] The Populist state treasurer, W. H. Worth, publicly and "heartily" seconded Thompson's views.[20] Populist newspapers also vigorously defended Thompson. Butler's *Caucasian,* for example, insisted that Thompson's stand could offend only those "whose attachment to the 'church' is more a result of fine sentiment than of actual knowledge."[21] A Rutherfordton Populist asserted that only the *"hired Plutocratic press"*

[17]Peter H. Argersinger, "Pentecostal Politics in Kansas: Religion, the Farmers' Alliance, and the Gospel of Populism, *Kansas Quarterly* 1 (1969): 24-35; Roscoe C. Martin, *The People's Party in Texas: A Study in Third Party Politics* (Austin, Texas, 1933), pp. 82-87; C. Vann Woodward, *Tom Watson, Agrarian Rebel* (New York, 1938), p. 138. For an interpretation that views Populist ideology as a reassertion of evangelical Protestant values in a time of severe social strain, see Roy Eugene Rice, "Religion, Ideology, and Change: A Study in the Traditionalistic Populism of William Jennings Bryan, 1896-1925" (Ph.D. diss., Harvard University, 1970).

[18]Z. E. DeWitt to Cyrus Thompson, Aug. 29, 1895, Thompson Papers, Southern Hist. Coll., UNC Lib.

[19]F. S. Blair to Thompson, Sept. 20, 1895, ibid.

[20]Charlotte *Observer,* Oct. 16, 1895.

[21]Sept. 5, 1895. See also excerpts from the Hickory *Mercury,* the Charlotte *People's Paper,* and the Concord *Vestibule,* all printed in the Raleigh *News and Observer,* Sept. 18, 1895.

defended the church and warned the *Biblical Recorder* to "bury [its] mouth in the dust and keep silent."[22]

The Populists could draw from ample evidence to show that many churchmen opposed any upsetting of the existing social order. The Charlotte *Observer* editorially endorsed a letter from a minister who tried to demonstrate that "sound money" was inseparable from "sound morality." He insisted that this logical exercise had "nothing to do with politics."[23] The pastoral solicitude of the Reverend J. D. Hufham, a Baptist, prompted him to denounce those politicians who "scared the people" by telling them that times were hard.[24] "The eagerness with which men in authority, both in Church and State, are subjected to criticism bodes no good for our country," added the *North Carolina Christian Advocate.*[25] E. A. Yates, a Methodist minister, replied to the charge that the churches had neglected their social responsibility by declaring that the church "is necessarily a conservative power . . ., an antagonist to all disorder. . . . It can but align itself with the powers that be, for 'they are ordained of God.'"[26] The Reverend John C. Kilgo proudly told a Durham audience that the church was free of "demagogues." It remained, he insisted, the "one hope of our salvation from the fury of the rabble and helplessness of the multitude."[27]

The response of many churchmen to the economic and social dislocation of the 1890s was meager indeed and lent additional weight to the Populist argument. The Baptist state convention, for example, regarded "hard times" only from the perspective of denominational self-interest. In 1894 it took official notice of low crop prices, but the only unfortunate result of this state of affairs seemed to be "the inability of some of our best people to give largely." The 1896 convention accused the "distracting political campaign" of contributing "no little to the falling off of our receipts."[28] Preachers often located the cause of economic hardship

[22]"A Baptist" to the Raleigh *Caucasian,* Oct. 10, 1895.

[23]June 30, 1895.

[24]Raleigh *Caucasian,* Dec. 3, 1896; Charlotte *Observer,* Nov. 15, 1896.

[25]Dec. 4, 1895.

[26]Yates to the Raleigh *News and Observer,* Sept. 22, 1895.

[27]Quoted, ibid., Sept. 21, 1894.

[28]*Minutes of the Annual Meeting of the Baptist State Convention of North Carolina . . . 1894,* p. 14; ibid. (1896), p. 16.

in a falling away from grace or in the immutable nature of human society. It was not the financial system, not the trusts, not any institutional failing that was to blame but rather, as the *North Carolina Presbyterian* put it, a "decadence in morals."[29] According to the Raleigh *Christian Advocate,* the state's poverty resulted "directly or indirectly from some transgression of divine law."[30] The *Biblical Recorder* was distressed by the "suffering in the land" but despaired of any remedy. "The poor ye have with you always," it concluded gravely.[31]

Believing as they did that sin lay at the root of North Carolina's troubles, many clergymen displayed little understanding of or sympathy with the Populists' demands for reform. The *Biblical Recorder* advised those "who are looking to legislation for relief to cease looking." What North Carolina needed was less selfishness and an increase in works of charity.[32] The Reverend Frank L. Reid, a Methodist, doubted the efficacy of "intellectual culture or legislation to cure our ills." Instead he urged Tarheels to devote more attention to "sound moral discipline in our churches." How else, he asked, unwittingly giving substance to Populist charges, could communism, nihilism, and the "many other pernicious isms" that hard times spawned be eradicated?[33] The *North Carolina Christian Advocate* maintained that whatever merit schemes of social reform might have, the church's purely spiritual mission precluded it from taking part in them. "Secular reforms," the paper pointed out, "have no place in the kingdom of heaven."[34]

Some preachers found it less difficult to incorporate a probusiness bias into the old framework of sin, grace, and salvation. The New South vision of industrial progress that emerged after Reconstruction had powerful evangelical potential and seemed to promise much more than just railroads and cotton mills. Preachers, like some secular propagandists, tended to identify traditional values and virtues with the goals of the New South, whose primary concern

[29] Mar. 19, 1896.

[30] Jan. 24, 1894.

[31] Jan. 24, 1894.

[32] July 11, Jan. 3, 1894.

[33] Reid, "The Duty and Destiny of the Church," in *Thirty Sermons by Thirty North Carolina Preachers,* ed. Levi Branson (Raleigh, 1893), pp. 233, 237.

[34] Mar. 20, 1895.

(at least rhetorically) was not profits but, according to Wilbur J. Cash, "the salvation of the decaying community." For example, the Reverend Wilbur Fiske Tillett, a professor of theology at Vanderbilt and a native of North Carolina, approved of the development of manufacturing because it resulted in the decrease of "public and private vices."[35] "Next to the grace of God," one minister told his congregation, "what Salisbury [North Carolina] needs is a Cotton Mill."[36]

Railroads, mines, and factories could become instruments of divine grace and means of regeneration if southern Protestantism seized its opportunity and accepted the challenge of the New South. Thomas Neal Ivey of the *North Carolina Christian Advocate* vividly described, albeit with much exaggeration, the changes taking place in the state:

This is an era of progress in our State. . . . Our population is rapidly increasing. Our towns and cities are growing. Where only a few years ago the virgin forests moaned, or the red gullies seamed the slopes, or the broomsedge waved their yellow plumes, are enterprising villages. . . . New industries are being opened. . . . Impatient locomotives are waiting for pick, drill and dynamite. . . . the smoke of cotton mills is blackening the sky that arches from the western peaks to the eastern sands.

But Ivey warned that under these circumstances the churches could not afford to let material progress overtake spiritual progress. He hoped that a vigorous Christianity would become "the chief glory" of the state's greatness.[37] Or, as the *Christian Educator* of Durham expressed it, "industrial development will not make a great people unless back of it is a great intellectual and spiritual life."[38] Churchmen were confident that this could happen in the South. The real difference between the North and the South, according to Methodist Bishop O. P. Fitzgerald, was that southerners "put God into [their] material progress." Henry Grady, he insisted, was no Jay

[35] Cash, *The Mind of the South* (New York, 1941), p. 182; Tillett, "The White Man and the New South," *Century Magazine* 33 (1887): 771-73.

[36] Quoted in Benjamin Burks Kendrick and Alex Matthews Arnett, *The South Looks at Its Past* (Chapel Hill, 1935), p. 125.

[37] Feb. 16, 1898.

[38] *Christian Educator* 1 (Feb. 1896): 1. See also *North Carolina Christian Advocate,* Mar. 9, 1898; *Biblical Recorder,* Jan. 1, 1896.

Gould.[39] But whether churchmen remained socially passive or became committed to a New South gospel, Populists who took comfort neither in traditional relationships nor in uncontrolled industrial development found the churches wanting.

Populist critics were convinced that the churches' social conservatism or probusiness bias stemmed in large part from a fear of alienating men of wealth. The *Caucasian* charged that the "leading" church members who would "howl" about mixing religion and politics (that is, politics aimed at social reform) were generally the men of substance in the community. "Too often," declared one Populist, "does the modern money changer and usurer pay the bulk of the preacher's salary." Another critic alleged that most preachers were "hypocrites and cowards," afraid to defy their wealthy parishioners.[40] Populists would not have been surprised to learn that the Reverend Mr. Reid, who denounced social reformers in the pages of the Raleigh *Christian Advocate,* was a man who could "mingle freely with businessmen" and who kept "in close touch with the commercial and industrial as well as the religious life of the community."[41]

The dependence of North Carolina churches upon the support of businessmen lent plausibility to Populist charges. Denominational drives to raise money for church buildings, colleges, orphanages, and missionary enterprises usually failed unless churchmen could convince men of means to make substantial contributions. Wake Forest and Trinity Colleges, for example, had a history of almost unrelieved financial crises until the last two decades of the nineteenth century, when the Baptists aroused the interest of James A. Bostick of New York in their plight and the Methodists secured the support of the Duke family of Durham.[42] When the Reverend Mr. Kilgo, the president of Trinity College, proclaimed publicly

[39]*Wesleyan Christian Advocate* (Atlanta), July 2, 1890.

[40]Raleigh *Caucasian,* June 6, 1895; "Church Member" to ibid.; Mrs. P. D. B. Arrington to Cyrus Thompson, Sept. 18, 1895, Thompson Papers. See also Thompson in the Raleigh *Caucasian,* Feb. 6, 1896; the Hickory *Mercury* quoted in the Raleigh *Progressive Farmer,* Sept. 10, 1895.

[41]From a letter quoted in N. H. D. Wilson, "The Reids: Eminent Itinerants through Three Generations," Trinity College *Historical Papers,* ser. 9 (Durham, 1912), p. 18.

[42]Daniels, p. 104; Earl W. Porter, *Trinity and Duke, 1892-1894: Foundations of Duke University* (Durham, 1964), pp. 1-53.

that "the free coinage controversy and such affairs was nonsense when we have built more factories in the South in the last twenty years than ever before," the *Caucasian* pointed to an obvious reason for this "gold bug speech": "a gentleman [Washington Duke] with strong gold bug characteristics has given Trinity College about $100,000 in all."[43]

A charge by Senator Butler that some North Carolina religious newspapers were controlled by the "trusts," though exaggerated, was not entirely without foundation.[44] Often suffering from a scarcity of funds, denominational newspapers in the South fought a hard struggle for survival. The Methodist press in North Carolina was no exception, and it welcomed the financial assistance that Benjamin Newton Duke generously provided. Ben Duke was a director of the American Tobacco Company, which his brother James Buchanan ("Buck") had organized, and the family was also involved in North Carolina railroads, banking, and textiles.[45] Ben Duke was a "loyal Methodist and patriotic citizen." In 1894 he paid the *Western Christian Advocate* of Asheville for twenty subscriptions, a number which the editor was anxious to see increased to fifty or one hundred. When a lack of funds forced Thomas N. Ivey to edit the *North Carolina Christian Advocate* and the Raleigh *Christian Advocate* for a year without salary, he was able to obtain a personal loan from Duke, who also granted him at least one extension on repayment. In addition, Duke was a stockholder in the Advocate Publishing Company, certainly an unprofitable investment financially speaking.[46]

The need for churches in the mushrooming mill villages of the piedmont provided the opportunity for arrangements advantageous both to money-starved denominations and to philanthropically minded manufacturers, some of whom regarded religion as a useful

[43] Raleigh *Caucasian,* July 18, 1895. Kilgo's speech was reported in the Raleigh *News and Observer,* July 3, 1895. See also Raleigh *Progressive Farmer,* June 18, 1895.

[44] Undated clipping in the Henderson Papers, Southern Hist. Coll., UNC Lib.

[45] For a sketch of B. N. Duke as well as information on his business activities, see *Biographical History of North Carolina,* ed. Samuel A. Ashe, 8 vols. (Greensboro, 1905-17), 3: 94-101.

[46] *Christian Educator* 1 (Dec. 1896): 1; P. L. Groome to B. N. Duke, Feb. 7, 1894, Ivey to Duke, June 7, 1899, L. W. Crawford to Duke, Jan. 6, 1899, Duke Papers, Duke Univ. Lib.

means of social control. In some villages the millowners deducted a certain amount from the operatives' wages in order to pay the pastors' salaries and to build churches. Mill managers sometimes served as Sunday school superintendents. One minister reported that the millowners "did not wish the thinking power of their operatives developed but did wish them to be very religious."[47] A Gastonia millowner insisted that all his employees attend some church—there is "no nagging of denominations," he declared—in order to insure that they would be "sober, moral, and virtuous hands."[48] Daniel A. Tompkins, a North Carolina manufacturer, earnestly recommended "a wholesome Christian invironment" for maintaining harmony and contentment among the operatives.[49] The state Bureau of Labor Statistics agreed. In its 1897 report on religious conditions in the mill villages it optimistically observed that the workers'

religious condition shows a decided improvement, for it appears as if, after the labor of a week, when Sunday comes it brings with it a change—a change from the physical labor of the past six days to rest on the seventh, and then, the mind being freed from the thoughts of the daily labor of the body, seeks delight in contemplating the beauties of nature and in listening to the voice of the Divine Master. The children on that day learn a lesson of love, for the Sunday-schools teach them of the way of life, of the pathway to eternity and they seem to associate the freedom of the day, with its rest from study or work, and the recreation of body and soul which they then enjoy, with the Divine goodness of the Giver.[50]

As long as religion merely refreshed the Sabbath, the millowners might feel confident that their "harmonious" relationship with workers would persist.

[47]Holland Thompson, *From Cotton Field to the Cotton Mill: A Study of the Industrial Transition in North Carolina* (New York, 1906), pp. 175-76. In a study of Gaston County, N.C., Liston Pope has thoroughly documented how the mills used the churches as agents of social control. See his *Millhands and Preachers: A Study of Gastonia* (New Haven, 1949), especially chaps. 3, 8, 9, 10.

[48]Charlotte *Observer*, Mar. 12, 1899.

[49]Tompkins to the Deaconess at High Shoals, Aug. 26, 1907, copy in the Tompkins Papers, Ms Div., Lib. Cong. See also Emmie G. Padgett to Tompkins, Mar. 10, 1896, and A. Q. Kale to Tompkins, Dec. 8, 1905, Tompkins Papers, Southern Hist. Coll., UNC Lib.

[50]*Eleventh Annual Report of the Bureau of Labor Statistics of North Carolina, Including the First Annual Report of the Inspector of Mines, for the Year 1897* (Raleigh, 1898), pp. 23-25.

The patronage of the wealthy, however altruistically intended, induced in many churchmen a sense of their own powerlessness, a fawning attitude, and a complacency toward social injustice. The Dukes represented paternalistic benevolence at its best, but their activities on behalf of North Carolina Methodism also revealed the pernicious effects of a relationship in which one side remained subordinate and dependent. Ben Duke and his father, Washington, enjoyed a well-deserved reputation for generosity, and requests for donations to build churches, pay pastors' salaries, buy organs, and support missionaries came to them in great volume. Ministers, deacons, and ladies' aid societies often couched their appeals in a language of abject desperation and mawkish humility.[51] Some of the brethren even sought spiritual guidance, particularly from the elder Duke, who was said to have a "child-like" faith.[52] One congregation invited him to attend a series of revival meetings and aid in improving "the spiritual condition of our body of believers." "We need your prayers and co-operation now," a lady of the church implored, "as much as we needed your previous gift."[53]

Few could equal the Dukes in their solicitude for the religious needs of the North Carolina factory population. Main Street Methodist Church in Durham (later Duke Memorial Church) was an outgrowth of a Sunday school in one of the Dukes' factories. Washington Duke donated the land and money for the building, served with his son Ben on its board, and even transferred his membership to the new congregation from the older and more prestigious Trinity Church. Washington Duke "could not accept the notion that social distinctions be carried into church life."[54] But outside the churches the distinctions remained. The poverty of the state's factory workers and their families prompted the pastors

[51]See, as examples of scores of such requests, J. C. Story to B. N. Duke, June 26, 1900, J. D. Andrew to B. N. Duke, Aug. 27, 1900, Mrs. M. B. Pitt to Washington Duke, Oct. 12, 1900, and J. S. Fox to Washington Duke, Oct. 15, 1900, Duke Papers.

[52]Robert W. Winston, *It's a Far Cry* (New York, 1937), p. 224. See also Josephus Daniels, *Tar Heel Editor* (Chapel Hill, 1939), p. 470; John C. Kilgo, *In Memory of Mr. Washington Duke: Exercises Held in Craven Memorial Hall, Trinity College, Durham, N.C., June 4, 1905* (n.p., n.d.).

[53]Mrs. W. T. Pearce to Duke, Sept. 23, 1896, Duke Papers.

[54]Kilgo, p. 21; Durham *Tobacco Plant*, Apr. 27, 1887 (photostat in Duke Univ. Lib.). Ben Duke provided the Methodists of West Durham, mostly operatives in the Erwin Cotton Mills (of which he was president), with both a lot and a church building ("Resolution of the West Durham Methodist Episcopal Church, South," Feb. 6, 1897, typescript in the Duke Papers).

to do little more than make additional supplications for aid from their benefactors. One minister informed Ben Duke that the Methodist church building at Proximity Mills near Greensboro had been completed almost a month before but was still encumbered by debt. He described his congregation's circumstances:

Our membership is about forty, all of whom have been received this year. Our members are all poor, there being no official of the mill connected with our church. We have succeeded in paying off all of the debt except two hundred dollars. Since you are vice-president of the mill, you are doubtless especially interested in their material welfare, and will be willing to help us raise the rest of the debt. Your large donations to other causes would keep us from expecting a very large sum from you, but since every nickel counts in a work among a people so poor as we are at Proximity, I feel sure that you will see fit to help us to some extent.

Duke noted on the letter: "Send $25.00."[55]

The Baptists were also concerned about conditions in the mill villages. The minutes of their 1899 convention contained a lengthy report on the movement of population from rural regions to new centers of manufacturing. Its only conclusion, however, was that the country Baptists were moving into areas of "pedobaptist" strength "where the influences are strong to undermine doctrinal conviction, finally resulting, unless remedy is provided, in an absolute loss from our strength." Hence the urgency to build churches. A year later the convention recognized the possibility of conflicts between capital and labor in the mill villages but implicitly offered consolation and encouragement to management by suggesting gravely that the "Gospel of Christ" would be "the best remedy and surest preventative of the bloodshed, arson and war."[56]

The interest that factory owners took in supporting the churches made the promise of the New South seem very real to many ministers and caused them to overlook the ugly social consequences of industrialization. Businessmen became the strong arm of the church in the drive for converts and membership. The Reverend F. A. Bishop, for example, urged Ben Duke to purchase a textile mill that

[55]Gilbert T. Rowe to Duke, Oct. 10, 1898, Duke Papers. See also D. N. Caviness to Duke, Apr. 28, 1899, ibid.

[56]*Minutes of the Annual Meeting of the Baptist State Convention of North Carolina* . . . 1899, pp. 26-27; ibid. (1900), p. 20.

was for sale near Fayetteville with "fine water power . . . and fix-tures—village buildings &c." Bishop considered it "essential that Methodist people should control it." Churchmen repaid their bene-factors with effusive public praise and stout defense of their activ-ities. The Reverend William L. Grissom, an editor of the *North Carolina Christian Advocate*, insisted that the average mill manager had "much to do with the social, moral and religious conditions" of the people and exercised a "wonderful influence over those who continually look to him for support and aid." The Reverend C. F. Sherrill denounced reformers who meddled in the affairs of the mill villages and condemned those who made any "invidious dis-tinction" that tended to "array the masses against the classes." He argued that "some of our noblest men, loving what is right and the cause of God, are at the head of the factories, giving employment to many who would be in wretched poverty and want." The good pastor concluded with the observation that "thousands of lazy people in our land piddling away at poor farms" would be "vastly better off . . . if they were at some good factory in full work."[57]

Thoughtful Populists were not content merely to denounce preachers for failing to advocate social reform. They went a step further and showed how the churches' acquiescence in the status quo had aided southern politicians in obfuscating many issues. The Democrats' exploitation of the race issue, their defense of traditional religion, and the churches' toleration of chattel slavery and later of "wage slavery" were for the Populist critics all part of the same process—mechanisms of class hegemony. "We often blush," admitted a Populist state legislator, W. R. Lindsay, "on reading many good papers and speeches, appealing in behalf of the poor, and urging the poor to better manners, to stop drink and debauchery, to go to Sunday school and attend church." "It seems," he went on, "that the two old parties will agree on the issues. The tariff and the 'nigger' seems to be the plan. . . . The churches will inveigh against the liquor traffic, and appeals to charitable objects, all running shy of hurting the money power."[58] In reply to a Baptist minister who claimed that his church had been a traditional opponent of oppression, Lindsay pointed out that Baptists had

[57] Bishop to Duke, Nov. 25, 1898, Duke Papers; *North Carolina Christian Advocate,* Jan. 13, 1896; Sherrill, ibid., Oct. 7, 1896.

[58] Lindsay in the Raleigh *Progressive Farmer,* Aug. 27, 1895.

tolerated human slavery in the South and thereby showed themselves "subject to social pressure and . . . all the PASSIONS AND PREJUDICES inherent in the society in which" they live.[59] Cyrus Thompson made the same point and added that the southern churches withdrew from the national denominations before the Civil War in order to be able to "live harmoniously" with a social system based on slavery. After the war the churches continued to accept the "lordship of Constantine" by supporting the "corporate interest" and showing little solicitude for the "masses [who] are impoverished, degraded and enslaved."[60]

The eagerness with which North Carolina's leading Democratic newspapers denounced Thompson and other critics of the churches indicated that the Populists had hit upon a politically sensitive issue. The Populists seemed to be trying to tear asunder the political and cultural fabric of the South for which old-fashioned Protestantism provided some crucial threads. Populists were well aware that the much revered but often abused doctrine of the spiritual nature of the church barely concealed the contentment of most preachers with the Old Order. The critics argued that the church's shunning of politics was nothing less than hypocrisy. Thompson attributed the retreat into spirituality in the face of "egregious wrongs" to the preachers' "subserviency and moral cowardice." "Forgetting that poverty is a disease more destructive than drunkness, they have," he charged, "affected to despise politics in their effort to save souls."[61] One Populist wrote of the preachers' "pious deceitfulness." Another made the following observation: "Let the preacher tell you about Jonah swallowing the whale, but don't ask him to condemn Cleveland and his administration. . . . The preacher says we have no business in politics; at the same time they are wielding a greater influence in that direction than any other set of men."[62]

Most preachers were probably not conscious hypocrites. Many of them found a passive (and sometimes active) acceptance of the status quo not only more congenial to their tastes than agitation

[59] T. H. Pritchard to the Raleigh *News and Observer*, Sept. 22, 1895; Lindsay in the Raleigh *Caucasian*, Oct. 24, 1895.

[60] Raleigh *Caucasian*, Feb. 6, 1896. See also the Hickory *Mercury* quoted in the Raleigh *Progressive Farmer*, Sept. 10, 1895.

[61] Raleigh *Caucasian*, Feb. 6, 1896.

[62] J. P. R. to ibid., July 4, 1895; R. H. W. Barker to ibid., June 20, 1895.

for change but morally more preferable. In fact old-time religion and old-line establishment politics were so closely identified in many clerical minds that to support the latter hardly seemed a violation of pure spirituality.[63] By its very nature hegemonic ideology tends to conceal the interrelationship between individual and institutional attitudes and roles, on the one hand, and the dominant interests in a society on the other. The Democrats, as the Populists realized, were quite ready to point to the church's attitude as a sanction for their party's legitimacy. The *Progressive Farmer* reprinted an editorial from the Democratic Smithfield *Herald* which revealed the intimate connection between preachers and the political establishment:

Johnston county is a Democratic county. . . . Even among our ministers are to be found some of our staunchest Democrats. Not long since we remember hearing a sermon . . . [in which] the good preacher paid a delicate yet direct compliment to the Democratic party. . . .

Among other things the minister in substance said: "I would warn the brethren against being led away by any new and strange doctrines either political or otherwise. Beware of the new 'isms.' Stand by the old ways. Be not allured by strange ideas. Stick by the old paths, and remove not the ancient landmarks which our fathers have set."[64]

In this way, then, some preachers could regard the Populist challenge as an "ism" just as harmful to the "old ways" (and implicitly the existing distribution of economic and political power) as, say, Darwinism or the higher criticism of the Bible. One Populist, however, had a simpler answer: "Most preachers," he complained, "are Democratic."[65]

The old party took comfort in preachers who "cling to the faith of their fathers."[66] But to the Democrats' dismay, Populist arguments seemed to have influenced some North Carolina preachers, leading them to question certain aspects of the status quo. As early

[63]For general observations on this point see H. Richard Niebuhr, *Christ and Culture* (New York, 1951), especially chap. 3, pp. 83-115. See also Will Herberg, *Protestant—Catholic—Jew: An Essay in American Religious Sociology* (rev. ed.; Garden City, N.Y., 1960); Sidney Mead, *The Lively Experiment: The Shaping of Christianity in America* (New York, Evanston, and London, 1963), pp. 134-55.

[64]Quoted in the Raleigh *Progressive Farmer*, May 21, 1895.

[65]Charles Eure to the Raleigh *Caucasian*, July 25, 1895.

[66]Raleigh *News and Observer*, Nov. 25, 1894.

as October 1894 Daniels expressed concern about this problem. The *News and Observer* accused Populists of intimidating preachers who did not join "their campaign of immorality and destruction." As proof that Populism had a "demoralizing effect" on ministers of the gospel, the Raleigh daily pointed to two preachers, elected as Populists to the legislature, who had allegedly been noticed "to walk rather unsteady, and to have an unnatural thickness of tongue, and irreverent breaths."[67] One of these preachers was John Ammons, a Baptist from Buncombe County. Active in founding many Baptist schools in the mountain region of the state, he had quit the Democratic party "in disgust" in 1890. The other clerical member was M. T. Lawrence of Martin County, a farmer and minister in the Primitive Baptist church, who was elected to two terms in the state house of representatives.[68] Although the *News and Observer* never proved its allegations against these two men, it concluded that it was "not perfectly safe for ministers to rub up against the corrupting environments of politics."[69] Not to be outdone, the conservative and usually more sedate Charlotte *Observer* heaped ridicule on a preacher, one Reverend Mr. Martin, who was a Populist candidate for the legislature from Mecklenburg County. It called him a "Pop. of the rankest order," "a man of profound ignorance, very nervous and excitable . . . with an Elgin-movement-clockworks system in the place where brains ordinarily are." Still, the *Observer* had to admit that the preacher brought to his task all the fervor of the evangelist, so that "the platform at times seems almost transformed into the pulpit, especially when he works 'round to the point where he says the present financial system is sending human souls to hell."[70]

In mid-1895 the Reverend P. L. Groome, the western editor of the *North Carolina Christian Advocate*,[71] began a searching criticism of the church's role in society that coincided with the Populist

[67] Oct. 31, 1894, Mar. 18, 1895.

[68] See the sketches of Ammons and Lawrence in Collins and Goodwin, *Biographical Sketches of the General Assembly of North Carolina* (Raleigh, 1895), pp. 23, 25.

[69] Mar. 15, 1895.

[70] Sept. 18, 1894.

[71] The *North Carolina Christian Advocate* had two editors, one from each of the two Methodist annual conferences in the state. This fact accounts for the paper's often conflicting editorial statements.

offensive against the traditional conservatism of southern Protestantism. Groome rejected the usual interpretation of the spiritual nature of the church, and until his sudden resignation in 1896 the editorial pages of the *Advocate* bristled with pronouncements that doubtless startled its more conservative readers. In June he asserted that banks "as a whole" favored the financial system least beneficial to the people. He suggested that legislators concerned with the public welfare should listen to what bankers advised and then do the opposite. Replying to criticism that his comments were "political" and for that reason violated the spirituality doctrine, Groome somewhat disingenuously denied that what he had said had political significance. "But," he added, "there is a great moral significance whether a great syndicate or congress of syndicates be allowed to fix or affect a financial basis by which many millions may be made to suffer." He endorsed an inflated currency not as an issue of politics but as "a vital interest of humanity."[72]

Groome also dared to question the benevolence of factory builders at a time when it was not fashionable for churchmen to do so. While Grissom, his coeditor on the *Advocate,* was praising the virtues of the cotton mills, Groome marshaled evidence showing that the mills were not unqualified blessings. He pointed out that lower wages and longer hours of labor prevailed in North Carolina than, for example, in Massachusetts. North Carolina had no compulsory education laws, nor did it prohibit or even limit child labor. Groome considered it "a momentous question for us as a people whether we will increase our wealth in enlargement and multiplication of plants, or increase the life force of our people by diminishing the hours of labor and provide enlarged public schools." He urged the state "as a moral person with responsibility to see that those unable to protect themselves shall have her protection." He demanded that the legislature lessen the hours of labor for all workers, enact compulsory education laws, and forbid child labor. When some churchmen questioned his position on state regulation, Groome answered, "we believe in applied Christianity and that the warfare against evil should be initiated by the Church and religious press, and be carried forward until the state acts."[73]

The Populists might have appreciated Groome's kind of applied Christianity, but the Democrats certainly did not. The Charlotte

[72]June 5, June 12, June 26, 1895. [73]Jan. 13, Jan. 20, Feb. 5, 1896.

Observer noted that many Methodists were "very much concerned" about Groome's editorials on money and bankers. "Two bank presidents here," it pointed out, "are among the most earnest Methodists in the State."[74] The *Observer* was in any case a "gold-bug" paper, but Daniels's *News and Observer,* although editorially endorsing such populistic measures as free silver, antitrust laws, and railroad regulation, fully agreed with its Charlotte contemporary about Groome. The *News and Observer* was the most influential Democratic daily in the state, and as much as Daniels would have liked to see all factions of the party converted to his neopopulist point of view, his chief concern was always Democratic victory, even when such an attitude played into the hands of conservatives.[75] When the welfare of the party was at stake, Daniels showed no mercy. He later admitted that the "paper was cruel in its flagellations. In the perspective of time, I think it was too cruel."[76] Daniels favored many of Groome's specific proposals for currency reform, but he probably realized that Groome's reformist editorials, de-spite—or indeed because of—their nonpolitical character, would benefit the Populist party, the only party in the state totally committed to reform. When Daniels took issue with Groome's aspersions on bankers, the preacher replied that he had no quarrel with them as individuals but only with the "money power" that "struck the demonetizing blow at silver." But Daniels was unsatisfied and made his real point by asking "whether it is wise for religious journals to enter upon a discussion of purely political questions."[77] The Democratic Concord *Times* frankly called Groom's editorials "Populistic."[78]

The Populist criticism of the churches provided Daniels with a unique opportunity to repair the damage caused by the state aid fight and to create a united front between preachers and Democrats against godless Populism. The *News and Observer* angrily charged that the Populist "crusade against the church" was "born of a spirit of iconoclasm that seeks to tear down every thing sacred." In his

[74]June 13, 1895.

[75]Winston, p. 209. See also Robert F. Durden, *Reconstruction Bonds and Twentieth Century Politics* (Durham, 1962), p. 10.

[76]Daniels, *Editor in Politics,* p. 145.

[77]Raleigh *News and Observer,* June 22, June 30, 1895; P. L. Groome to ibid., June 28, 1895.

[78]Quoted in Reidsville *Webster's Weekly,* June 7, 1895.

editorial columns Daniels challenged the Populists to show that North Carolina preachers represented anything less than "the best thought, the loftiest patriotism, the sweetest charity, and the truest benevolence." He accused Populist leaders of trying to "crush the powers of the preachers" because the church had refused to bow down to Populist materialism and "worship the dollar."[79]

Daniels even organized in the *News and Observer* a "symposium" of prominent churchmen to discuss Thompson's "famous remark" that the church supported "human slavery." But he had no intention of promoting an objective discussion on the issue. "I think it exceedingly important," he wrote to one of the participants, "that the clergy of the State should rebuke this attempt to bring the church into disrepute."[80] Daniels's symposium appeared to be successful. The eight clergymen who contributed to it expressed their disagreement with Thompson with varying degrees of emphasis. Almost every contributor paid tribute to the spiritual nature of the church, but one preacher's reference to the Populists as "anarchists and communists" indicated that it was not a doctrine to be narrowly construed. An extract from the Atlanta *Constitution,* which Daniels printed in the same issue in which the symposium appeared, made the Democratic position quite clear: "Our people, left to themselves, without the influence and restraints of the church, would yield to the spirit of selfishness and greed, and they would soon defy human laws and plunge the land into strife." It would be difficult to find a more forthright defense than this of the role that "spiritual" churches were expected to play in preserving class hegemony.[81]

The Populists charged that the Democratic defense of the church was a politically motivated attempt to discredit their party. They insisted that Democratic professions of piety were thinly disguised appeals to churchmen who might otherwise have concluded that the church had made "some rather bad alliances" with the old party.[82] In a concise summary of the Thompson affair the *Caucasian* gave the Populist interpretation of the controversy:

[79]Raleigh *News and Observer,* Sept. 8, Sept. 18, 1895.

[80]Josephus Daniels to John C. Kilgo, Sept. 17, 1895, Trinity College Papers, Duke Univ. Archives.

[81]Raleigh *News and Observer,* Sept. 22, 1895.

[82]Raleigh *Caucasian,* Sept. 26, 1895.

It sometimes proves unfortunate for a man to be more intelligent than the mass of people among whom he lives. When he ventured the assertion that the Church was on the side of human slavery, he was attacked by the Democratic press. THAT press didn't know nor did it care whether Dr. Thompson was right or not. It thought it could injure Dr. Thompson by appealing to the prejudice and ignorance of a certain element of people who are more "reverent" than intelligent, and it sought to injure him and the Alliance by such an appeal to that class of people.[83]

The Populists, then, the party of unlettered "anarchists," were able to brand the Democrats, the party of "virtue" and "intelligence," as antiintellectual, hypocritical, and panderers to the prejudices of the masses.

The symposium also triggered sharp responses from two of the state's leading clergymen, Columbus Durham and John C. Kilgo, both of whom were unsympathetic to Populism. Daniels had invited Durham to participate in his symposium, apparently hoping to score a point against the Populists by enlisting the support of his old enemy in the state aid fight against Thompson's attack on the preachers. Durham did write an article, but the *News and Observer* failed to publish it. It soon appeared in the Populist press. According to a bold headline in the *Caucasian*, "IT DIDN'T FIT THE CASE."[84] "The clergy of North Carolina," Durham exclaimed, "are not a set of holy noodles, or sanctified doodles, to be frightened on the one hand by a reckless statement of an Onslow doctor or humbugged on the other side by the insidious plans of a political editor." "Remember too, Joe," he concluded, "you returned from Washington City 'to save the State,' and not 'the Church'; and you haven't saved the State yet."[85] Although Durham's acid pen spared neither Thompson nor Daniels, the Populists must have reasoned that their side would reap the greater advantage by printing his article. Durham was, after all, a Democrat of unimpeachable standing, and yet he was now attacking one of the key leaders in the fight to "save the State" from fusion rule. Moreover, Durham's article only condemned Thompson's views, whereas it attacked Daniels's motives. Thompson, Durham was

---

[83]Feb. 6, 1896.   [84]Oct. 3, 1895.

[85]Ibid.; Raleigh *Progressive Farmer,* Oct. 1, 1895.

careful to point out, had made a "reckless statement"; Daniels was laying "insidious plans."

Kilgo's contribution to the symposium was more subtle—at least subtle enough for the *News and Observer* to print it. His was the only article to appear that shifted the debate from a criticism of Thompson and the Populists to a questioning of Daniels's motives. "Speakers at college commencements," Kilgo declared, obviously referring to defenders of university appropriations, "denounce the church as narrow, bigoted and sectarian. Men write down Christian colleges as 'sectarian fanaticism,' and occasionally editors denounce the ministry. . . . Of them all, Dr. Thompson is most innocent, though I must condemn any erroneous attack that the Doctor intended." Durham immediately perceived where the burden of Kilgo's criticism lay, and he jubilantly wrote his Methodist colleague: "Of all whose articles were printed you seem to have been the only one who understood the invidious plans of the Editor to use the preachers, without their knowledge, for political ends." Some churchmen, then, were repelled by what they considered blatant Democratic hypocrisy. The Charlotte *Observer* complained that Thompson's "outrageous libel" had "excited practically no indignation at all" on the part of the clergy.[86] In fact the state's denominational press maintained a studied silence throughout most of the controversy. From the Democrats' point of view that was spirituality with a vengeance.

[86]Raleigh *News and Observer,* Sept. 22, 1895; Durham to Kilgo, Sept. 27, 1895, Trinity College Papers; Charlotte *Observer,* Sept. 24, 1895.

IV

John C. Kilgo and the Disruption
of North Carolina Methodism

ONE PURPOSE of Josephus Daniels's anti-Thompson symposium was to tighten the embrace of the Democratic party around churchmen otherwise alienated by the state aid controversy and the Populist upheaval. Daniels was equally anxious that the Methodist college president John C. Kilgo not use his influence on behalf of the Baptist efforts against state aid. As a genuine friend of the university and as an active Methodist layman, Daniels also had a personal stake in the matter. He knew that a sizable element in the Methodist church strongly favored a continuation of appropriations to the university. In 1894, for example, the *North Carolina Christian Advocate* could "not see any ground whatever for a campaign against the state schools,"[1] and the Baptists did not fail to take the Methodists to task for their coolness toward the struggle.[2] When Kilgo became president of Trinity College in August 1894, Daniels was one of a number of Methodists who urged him to stay clear of the state aid issue. "I have run the risk of giving advice unsought and possibly winning your disapproval by this letter," he wrote, "but I am so anxious for your success in the State . . . that I run the risk of expressing to you my conviction of what is best for you, the church, and the State."[3]

Kilgo was a native of South Carolina who served his church there first as a circuit rider and then as financial secretary for Wofford College. His reputation as a religious and educational leader and most importantly as a vigorous advocate for a struggling, financially insecure church institution led to his call to the presidency of Trinity, where he remained until becoming a bishop in 1910.[4]

[1]Aug. 8, 1894; see also Apr. 18, Aug. 1, 1894.

[2]*Biblical Recorder,* Jan. 23, 1895.

[3]Daniels to Kilgo, Sept. 22, 1894, Kilgo Papers, Duke Univ. Archives. See also R. S. Webb to Kilgo, Aug. 2, 1894, and Robert C. Durham to Kilgo, Aug. 13, 1894, ibid.

[4]Paul Neff Garber, *John Carlisle Kilgo, President of Trinity College, 1894-1910* (Durham, 1937), pp. 1-16 and passim.

Kilgo did not openly join the Baptists in 1894 either because he had not yet made up his mind or because he felt he first had to get his bearings in a new state. The enthusiastic response given by students and faculty to Kilgo when he preached at the university late in 1894 must have encouraged friends of that institution to think it might gain his support.[5] Still, a month earlier he had written privately that he did "not believe in *free* higher education by church or state."[6] Then in January 1895 he published an article in the *Advocate* in which he insisted that.the state could not provide true Christian education.[7] The reaction of one Democratic newspaper was prophetic: "They [the Baptists] say that while he has not absolutely committed himself to their cause, his recent article in the *Christian Advocate* shows that he will soon be with them."[8]

Years later Daniels wrote that he was "soon made to feel" that his early advice to Kilgo not to oppose the university "was not agreeable—that it was in fact resented."[9] Daniels must have gotten a sense of this resentment from Kilgo's contribution to the anti-Thompson symposium in September. The symposium may also have marked a turning point for Kilgo. The Democratic editor's efforts to use the preachers for political ends underscored the danger, as Kilgo saw it, of mixing politics and education at the state university. When in November 1895 the *News and Observer* reasserted its claim as defender of the faith by again listing those preachers who had participated in the symposium, it omitted Kilgo's name.[10] The following January, Kilgo established the monthly *Christian Educator* at Durham to serve as the Methodist propaganda vehicle against state aid. During the next two years he traveled throughout the state speaking at Methodist churches on behalf of the cause.

Controversy always followed close on Kilgo's heels. Although he was an eclectic and sometimes contradictory thinker, he was also a

[5]Raleigh *News and Observer,* Nov. 15, 1894.

[6]Kilgo to [?], Oct. 10, 1894, copy in the Trinity College Papers, Duke Univ. Archives.

[7]Jan. 9, 1895.

[8]Reidsville *Webster's Weekly,* Jan. 17, 1895.

[9]Josephus Daniels, *Editor in Politics* (Chapel Hill, 1941), p. 113.

[10]Nov. 3, 1895.

bold and brilliant propagandist. He had received only two years of college training and has been described as "the rough and ready type; a man of action rather than a man of thought."[11] Kilgo held his convictions deeply, and he rarely hesitated to express them—or to impose them. His dominating, at times arrogant, personality could arouse either intense dislike or deep affection. There was usually no middle ground. His brother James doubted if Kilgo had ever preached a sermon or delivered an address "that did not result in dividing the crowd. Some would cry, 'Away with him,' and others, 'We shall hear him again.' Fact is, all returned to hear him."[12] Professor John Spencer Bassett of Trinity described Kilgo as "a man of striking originality," "deeply religious without being dogmatic, and practical without being mechanical," as one "singularly free from party bitterness." To Daniels, on the other hand, he came to represent all that was "false, absurd, fantastical, egotistical, malicious." Opposition to state aid was only a part of what Daniels called "Kilgoism."[13] The president of Trinity had pronounced views on a number of issues which in the turbulent nineties stirred controversy both within and outside of the Methodist church. His frankness in speaking on broad social questions having apparently little to do with the salvation of the soul and the nurture of the mind often invited the complaint that he failed to heed the limitations which a spiritual church placed upon its clergy. Taken together, Kilgo's actions posed difficult problems for the building of a solid Methodist phalanx behind him. Yet he applied to his task all of the fervor and energy that characterized the most successful practitioners of his clerical calling.

Kilgo's opposition to state aid did not grow out of the sense of powerlessness and frustration that may have motivated many Baptists. The New South vision of progress under the beneficent guidance of businessmen had grasped his imagination and strongly influenced his conception of Christian education. Like Walter Hines Page and other progressive critics of southern traditionalism, Kilgo was convinced that old institutions, old ways of thinking about

[11]Undated ms. in the Boyd Papers, Duke Univ. Archives.

[12]Quoted in Garber, p. 7. For the typically divided reaction of one congregation, see the Sanford *Express* quoted in the Wilmington *Messenger*, Aug. 3, 1897.

[13]Bassett, "John Carlisle Kilgo," in *Biographical History of North Carolina*, ed. Samuel A. Ashe, 8 vols. (Greensboro, 1905-17), 1: 351, 352, 355; Raleigh *News and Observer*, Dec. 17, 1903.

problems, and the provincial mentality had to be overcome if the South was to keep step with the rest of the nation in the development of a modern industrial civilization. The South, he believed, was just emerging from the primitive stage of its development. Apparently finding social Darwinism congenial to Methodist perfectionism, Kilgo pictured society evolving slowly from "degraded brutalism" through higher planes of development toward "divine life." He emphasized that man reached the fullness of his possibilities through increased awareness and self-consciousness.[14] The South, he asserted, remained more backward than the rest of the country largely because institutions, or the absence of them, encouraged an emotionalism uncongenial to the development of a rational and controlled intelligence. Progress depended primarily upon the "social sentiments" of the people. He explained that politicians, editors, teachers, lecturers, and preachers wishing to influence southern opinion and conduct appealed to the "emotional sentiments." Kilgo pointed to "a well-known law of psychology" which taught that thought and emotion were mutually antagonistic. "A well-established emotionalism," he added, "tends to put one out of sympathy with intellectualism."[15]

Kilgo maintained that the two agencies best suited to promote proper social ideals in the South were the colleges and the churches. Both had failed in large measure. But at Trinity he hoped to set a standard, to provide a model, by encouraging "Christian education." He intended that "the tides of national thought must sweep through the institution."[16] He chided the opponents of his conception of Christian education for believing that the church dealt only with "religious emotions and states." Ideally the church, the agency of the kingdom of God, was concerned with every aspect of human life. Education similarly involved the whole man. Thus the two were eminently compatible.[17] In fact, only an education which assumed *"Christ's estimate of all*

[14] Kilgo, "An Exalted Regard of Man, the Basis of True Social Progress," *Christian Educator* 1 (May 1896): 1.

[15] Kilgo, "Some Phases of Southern Education," *South Atlantic Quarterly* 2 (1903): 142, 143.

[16] Undated ms. in the Boyd Papers.

[17] Kilgo, *Christian Education: Its Aims and Superiorities* (Durham, 1896), p. 1.

things" could properly inculcate *"the fundamental truths of personal and social character."*[18] At Trinity, Christian education did not mean just "reading the Bible and the offering of prayers every day"; rather, the college's mission was to "enlarge Christianity into a vast system of life."[19] Rejecting the doctrine of the spiritual nature of the church, Kilgo demanded that the church and the college broadcast their convictions on politics, society, and government. "To show a selfish indifference to the problems of human progress," he warned, "is an act of treason to the interests of mankind that is only increased in its shamefulness by the exalted position of those who perpetrate it."[20] He invoked divine pity upon the typical southern preacher, a "soft brained and conscienced little carcass, wrapped up in a clerical coat going around in the land pretending to preach the Gospel of God."[21]

Under Kilgo's leadership Trinity developed into an institution that incorporated many of the latest innovations in higher education and followed the most fashionable intellectual trends. "The Church," he declared, "dishonors Christ when it trembles before any new propositions of science or literary critics [i.e., biblical criticism]." He accused the church, for example, of "a blind assault rashly made" on Darwinism.[22] Professor Bassett believed that Trinity was wholly free "from the influence of political and other prejudices" and a "leader of thought" in the state.[23] During his administration Kilgo raised admission requirements, modernized an antiquated curriculum, and continued his predecessor's policy of encouraging the faculty to seek graduate training. By 1898 half of the teaching staff was at least in the process of gaining doctoral degrees and two-thirds had received some graduate instruction.[24]

Trinity College became a major center for the propagation of the capitalist ideals of the New South. In terms of a traditional

[18]*Chapel Talks by John Carlisle Kilgo*, ed. D. W. Newsom (Nashville, 1922), p. 53.

[19]Kilgo in the Raleigh *News and Observer*, Nov. 12, 1895.

[20]*Chapel Talks*, pp. 53, 68.

[21]"Dr. Kilgo's Sermon before the Student Body at Main Street Church, Sunday Morning, Sept. 18 [no year]," ms. in the Kilgo Papers.

[22]"Annual Opening Sermon Preached by Dr. John C. Kilgo before the Student Body of Trinity College, Sept. 17, 1899," typescript, ibid.

[23]Quoted in Nannie M. Tilley, *The Trinity College Historical Society, 1892-1941* (Durham, 1941), p. 58.

[24]Earl W. Porter, *Trinity and Duke, 1892-1894: Foundations of Duke University* (Durham, 1964), pp. 70-77.

southern contempt for the enterprising Yankee and all his works, New South apostles like Henry Grady seemed to be offering something quite new. Priding himself on his progressive ideas, Kilgo embraced the new ethic wholeheartedly. He insisted that *"the new South must be a national South."*[25] In an address on "American Commercialism," he set forth the firm belief that the future of civilization in the South depended on the extent of the region's industrialization. He denounced "the zealots who seek to transfer industry and business success from the list of virtues to the catalogue of vices . . . [and have] a tramp for a moral ideal, and a country poor-house for the highest mark of civilization." Kilgo insisted that industrialization had benefited American culture profoundly. He praised the unselfish philanthropy of industrial leaders and rejoiced that "we are owning and developing our brotherhood in the roar of machinery and ring of the hammer."[26]

Trinity's progressivism did not entail much sympathy for the grievances of those for whom the New South meant only new kinds of economic exploitation. The views of Jerome Dowd, professor of political economy, revealed the tension at the college between newer and older ways of thinking about the relevance of Christianity to society. Dowd liked to use the fashionable vocabulary of the social gospel, studded with the jargon of sociology, but he had difficulty in squaring it with his distrust of social reform. For example, he urged preachers who wanted to free themselves from "an individualistic conception of Christianity" to study sociology and economics and to read the works of certain writers on Christian social ethics. But he then went on to warn that some recent writers—the very ones he had recommended—"go beyond the scope of Christianity." "For instance, Dr. [Richard] Ely would have preachers to advocate certain laws for the protection of children and Dr. [Washington] Gladden would have them to champion municipal ownership of public works, and Mr. [George] Herron seeks to impress the idea that Christianity justifies a general scheme of cooperation or socialism."[27] Dowd reflected the hostile attitude at Trinity toward any kind of alteration of capitalist institutions

[25]Undated typescript in the Kilgo Papers.

[26]Kilgo, *American Commercialism: An Address* (Durham, 1902), pp. 2, 3, 10, 15. See also Kilgo, "William H. Branson," Trinity College *Historical Papers*, ser. 4 (Durham, 1900), p. 25; *Chapel Talks*, pp. 80-81.

[27]Dowd, "Christianity and Social Science," *Christian Educator* 1 (Mar. 1896): 1.

and social relations. The college, declared Kilgo's *Christian Educator*, "has no sympathy with, or confidence in, those ideas and methods of reform and improvement that would reform the State instead of the individual Citizen, that would improve parties by forming new ones out of the same unimproved members of old ones and that would reform schools instead of reforming students."[28] Kilgo spoke of "immutable" economic laws and waxed eloquent about the character-building powers of poverty.[29] For the hard-pressed farmer he counseled patience, frugality, hard work, and honesty. "Cheap cotton," he added, "does not demand a cheap sense of duty."[30]

The ideas of Kilgo and his professors conformed to the class interests of those who wanted to create in North Carolina a favorable climate for capitalist enterprise. However, the political turmoil of the 1890s seemed calculated to hinder their efforts. Politics in North Carolina, Kilgo insisted, "inspired hatreds, nursed jealousies, fostered sectionalisms, petted intolerances, fired racial antagonisms, mocked the pulpit, belittled the church, paralyzed industry, wrecked business, excused lying, engaged in thefts, defended murders, joined fortunes with gamblers and liquor vendors, and set God at naught with contemptuous freedom."[31] He denounced "partisan and passion provoking journalism"; he criticized political "quack healers" who "cow like slaves before popular insanity."[32] The people, he maintained, could not find the cure for their poverty in politics; moreover, the platforms of all parties "meant the same thing."[33] Christian education, whatever else it involved, was supposed to develop the solid virtues that led to business success. Secular higher education in Germany and in the United States, he believed, fostered socialism; the Christian education offered by Trinity, however, promoted "the best kind of patriotism and citizenship."[34]

---

[28]1 (Feb. 1896): 1. In some ways the views expressed at Trinity were similar to what Henry F. May has called conservative social Christianity (*Protestant Churches and Industrial America* [New York, 1949], pp. 164-68).

[29]*Chapel Talks*, pp. 17-18; Kilgo, "Baccalaureate Address," *Christian Educator* 1 (June 1896): 1.

[30]*Chapel Talks*, p. 151.   [31]Quoted in Garber, p. 179.

[32]*Chapel Talks*, p. 146; quoted in the *Christian Educator* 2 (June 1897): 1.

[33]*Webster's Weekly*, Apr. 15, 1897.

[34]Kilgo, *Christian Education*, p. 5.

Kilgo's close association with businessmen and Trinity's location in Durham—a New South boomtown—go far toward explaining the college's class orientation. Durham was the home of Julian S. Carr, John C. Angier, George W. Watts, W. A. Erwin, and the Dukes, men who made their fortunes after the Civil War in the manufacture of tobacco and textiles. The wealthy citizens eagerly supported the building of schools, libraries, hospitals, churches, and other institutions that any community convinced of its future greatness had to possess.[35] The *Christian Educator* praised the substantial men of the town for displaying "the same energy and enthusiasm in religious and literary matters that they do in industrial affairs." Professor Bassett believed that "the force of industrialism" in Durham would change "the whole intellectual outlook of the people." His experiences in Durham, he wrote in 1911, had made him hopeful for the future of the "new regime." "Still in a rather new state," it had progressed through "a natural process, making money first, establishing a new ruling class, a class of wealth and power, and intelligence." Like Kilgo, Bassett had no patience with the "holy element of the church," which presumably impeded progress.[36] Here in Durham, then, was the ideal place for that synthesis Kilgo envisioned of religion, education, and industrialism that would transform the South.[37]

Two of the leading national propagandists of New South progressivism, Walter Hines Page and William Garrott Brown, found the situation both in Durham and at Trinity quite congenial to their tastes. Both men corresponded regularly with members of the Trinity faculty and were made welcome at the college.[38] The "hubbub" that Page's denunciations of the popular religion raised

[35] For an account of such developments in Durham, see William Kenneth Boyd, *The Story of Durham, City of the New South* (Durham, 1925).

[36] *Christian Educator* 3 (Feb. 1898): 1; J. S. Bassett, "How Industrialism Builds Up Education," *World's Work* 8 (1904): 5030; Bassett to Henry G. Connor, Aug. 12, 1911, Connor Papers, Southern Hist. Coll., UNC Lib.; Bassett to Herbert B. Adams, Nov. 15, 1898, *Historical Scholarship in the United States, 1876-1901: As Revealed in the Correspondence of Herbert B. Adams,* ed. W. Stull Holt (Baltimore, 1938), p. 256.

[37] What gave Durham its modern character were "the church, the school, and the factory" (Boyd, p. 132).

[38] On Page and Trinity, see Porter, pp. 98, 115, and 128. See also the correspondence between Page and Edwin Mims in the Page Papers, Houghton Lib., Harvard Univ., and the extensive correspondence between Brown and William Preston Few in the Few Papers, Duke Univ. Archives.

in North Carolina did not seem to damage his relationship with the men at the Methodist college.[39] Edwin Mims, professor of English, assured Page of his "belief in the new order of things" and supported the latter's "attack on the church." When Page called for a "wiser statesmanship and a more certain means of grace" in his "Forgotten Man" address at Greensboro in 1897, Kilgo publicly proclaimed it "one of the greatest speeches ever delivered in the State" and endorsed "every word of it."[40] Page, for his part, praised Trinity's "standard for scholarship" and its devotion to "the high culture of men."[41]

William Garrott Brown, like Page an expatriate southerner, also believed that the advancement of civilization followed closely on the heels of industrial progress. Pointing out that preachers were often "an entirely unprogressive and even reactionary influence," Brown placed ultimate blame for the South's backwardness on the inherited social conditions of the people and "the temper of the community." What was needed was a change of ideals which would come when the pursuit of wealth became "a passion." Industrialism would "awaken" the people and "waste, extravagance, self-indulgence, laziness, contempt for work—these old-time habits" would disappear. In Durham, Brown discovered an excellent example of the change he was advocating. Here was "less bigotry and more tolerance" than anywhere else in the South; the town's "new industrialism and commercialism . . . proved to be the strongest impulse toward liberalism ever awakened in North Carolina."[42]

Perhaps one of the most important influences shaping the outlook of Kilgo and Trinity was the close personal relationship that developed between the former circuit rider and the Duke family, the college's chief benefactor. When Kilgo came to Trinity in 1894,

[39]On the criticism of Page in North Carolina, see Burton J. Hendrick, *The Life and Letters of Walter Hines Page*, 2 vols. (New York, 1922), 1: 80; Edwin Mims, *The Advancing South* (New York, 1926), pp. 33-34. For an example of the criticism, see the *Presbyterian Standard* (Charlotte), June 19, July 10, 1901.

[40]Mims to Page, April 12, 1902, Page Papers; Page, *The Rebuilding of Old Commonwealths* (New York, 1902), p. 26; Kilgo quoted in the Raleigh *News and Observer,* July 15, 1897.

[41]Quoted in Garber, p. 137. Page also had kind words for Ben Duke; see Page to Willia Alice Page, Feb. 17, 1899, Page Papers.

[42]"Stanton" [William G. Brown] in the Boston *Evening Transcript,* Feb. 27, Mar. 9, 1904.

Washington Duke, the patriarch of the clan, was becoming disillu-
sioned with the prospects of the college, for the church seemed
unwilling to make the necessary sacrifices to keep the institution
on a sound financial footing. But Kilgo made a favorable impression
on "old Wash," who admired the president's business acumen.
Benjamin Duke marveled at Kilgo's ability to "stretch" a dollar.
Furthermore, the elder Duke, an old-fashioned Methodist, liked a
good preacher—and that Kilgo certainly was. The old man embraced the young college president "as one of his most intimate
spiritual advisors."[43] According to Daniels, Washington Duke "was
fond of telling people that Dr. Kilgo was the greatest preacher and
the most wonderful man who had ever come to North Carolina."[44]
"I have never felt so confident about the future of Trinity College
as I do at present," Ben Duke wrote to a friend. "I am sure that the
hand of God must have been in Kilgo's selection."[45]

There was an apparent contradiction between Kilgo's commitment to the New South and his seemingly reactionary opposition
to state aid to the university. Kilgo was trying to develop Trinity
into an institution appropriate to the needs of modern society,
but he never lost his faith in the individualistic virtues of laissez-
faire capitalism and the moral imperatives of a Christianity appropriate to it. The church was still supposed to provide the cohesive
elements to hold the community together. "The state may assume
to educate," he wrote, "but its inability to deal with the profound
truths and principles of Christian character, and its undetermined
system of morals unfits it for the work of true education."[46]
One of the principal dangers of state higher education, according
to Kilgo, was its tendency to undermine the energetic capitalism
that the South seemed so desperately to need. "With all the progress of educational facilities," he declared, "we have more tramps
to-day than ever before. Educated Germany is crowded with Communists and anarchists."[47] The university's policy of offering free
scholarships had a particularly damaging effect on character. The

[43] Garber, pp. 89-90.

[44] P. 118.

[45] Quoted in Porter, p. 59.

[46] Quoted in Garber, p. 13. See also Kilgo, *Christian Education.*

[47] Kilgo, "Religious Education and Social Reform," *Christian Educator* 1 (May
1896): 1.

poor boy needed no "coddling at the hands of any one."[48] Colleges were not supposed to be "educational pauper houses." They were not supposed to develop "socialistic notions."[49] Kilgo's principal argument against state aid was that the appropriations were being wasted on free scholarships.

Kilgo's activities exacerbated a Methodist factionalism which partly predated his arrival in North Carolina. His efforts to implement his policies were seriously endangered by it. John Franklin Crowell, Kilgo's predecessor, believed that his effectiveness as president of Trinity had been seriously impaired by the "factional discord . . . [which] had developed a pronounced condition of bad feeling among brethren usually supposed to dwell together in unity." The Reverend Mr. Grissom of the *North Carolina Christian Advocate* wondered why North Carolina Methodists could not unite on church enterprises as easily as Methodists of other states. "It is a sad fact," he lamented, ". . . that the N.C. Conference has been almost a continual battlefield from the time that it was set off as such down to the present." Some of the Methodist bickering and infighting was of that petty and parochial kind which lent substance to Page's observation that southern religious partisanship gave one a "sense of suffocation."[50] But legitimate problems of disaffected elements in the church as well as class tensions also contributed much to the Methodists' difficulties.

In large part Methodist discord reflected the long-standing antagonism between the East and the West in North Carolina. As President Crowell observed, the two sections "constitute two quite distinct domains of civic consciousness."[51] Attempts to alleviate sectional tension in the church led in 1890 to the division of North Carolina Methodism into two annual conferences: the North Carolina Annual Conference in the East and the Western North Carolina

[48]Kilgo, "Baccalaureate Address," ibid. 1 (June 1896): 1.

[49]Kilgo, "Education of the Poor Boy," ibid. 1 (Aug. 1896): 1. This article appeared also in the *Biblical Recorder,* July 15, 1896, and originally in the Charlotte *Observer,* June 10, 1896.

[50]Crowell, *Personal Recollections of Trinity College, North Carolina, 1887-1894* (Durham, 1939), p. 234; ms. address (1896) in the William L. Grissom Papers, Duke Univ. Lib.; Page to Robert C. Ogden, Dec. 17, 1903, copy in the Page Papers.

[51]Crowell, p. 103. On North Carolina sectionalism, see Guion Griffis Johnson, *Ante-Bellum North Carolina: A Social History* (Chapel Hill, 1937), pp. 31-36; and V. O. Key, Jr., *Southern Politics in State and Nation* (New York, 1949), pp. 218-23.

Annual Conference. The line dividing the two ran through the heart of the piedmont about halfway between Greensboro and Durham in a northeasterly-southwesterly direction. Unfortunately division served only to intensify sectional animosities, especially after Trinity College, which remained under the control of both conferences, moved from a rural location in Randolph County in the western conference to the town of Durham in the eastern. In addition, the oldest and most important Methodist newspaper in the state, the Raleigh *Christian Advocate,* became the official organ of the eastern conference but continued to enjoy wide circulation in the West—to the disadvantage of smaller western papers. One of the editors of the Raleigh paper, the Reverend David Atkins, was even a member of the western conference.[52]

Trinity College undoubtedly benefited by moving from a relatively isolated location in the western piedmont to rapidly growing Durham. But the move inflicted wounds in the western conference that did not quickly heal. Understandably the villagers at Old Trinity and the inhabitants of the surrounding counties "were almost unanimous in their opposition" to the move, and some faculty opposed it. Most members of the western conference were at best unenthusiastic about it.[53] After 1892 Trinity High School, a preparatory school under the control of the college's board of trustees, occupied the old buildings. There was no little anxiety in the western conference that Old Trinity would founder because of neglect by the board.[54] Crowell hoped to assuage western fears by developing Old Trinity, along with two other small institutions in the western conference, into two-year junior colleges whose graduates could then enter the third-year class at Trinity. The latter would become a true university with graduate and professional schools.[55] But Crowell's ideas did not suit Kilgo's purposes, for the new president wanted to centralize the church's educational work in Durham. Kilgo's administration proved indifferent to the welfare of the high school, and soon the Trinity board of trustees simply

[52]The details of the conference division can be found in the Raleigh *Christian Advocate* for 1890.

[53]Nora C. Chaffin, *Trinity College, 1839-1892: The Beginnings of Duke University* (Durham, 1950), p. 479; Crowell, pp. 68, 146.

[54]*North Carolina Christian Advocate,* June 6, 1894. See also L. W. Crawford to J. F. Heitman, Nov. 2, 1893, Trinity College Papers.

[55]Crowell, pp. 82-83.

refused to continue to subsidize it. The hostile reaction in the West was hardly surprising.[56]

The sectional controversy over Trinity College became entangled in a so-called newspaper war centering on disputes over the control and policy of the Methodist press in North Carolina. After the conference division in 1890, considerable sentiment favored the establishment of a joint organ for East and West in order to end the ruinous competition between the Raleigh *Christian Advocate* and the *Western Christian Advocate*—a contest which had been causing "bitterness and strife among the brethren."[57] Late in the fall of 1893 the two conferences agreed in principle on consolidation, "if," as the report of the eastern conference stated, "it can be done peaceably and successfully."[58] In February 1894 a joint commission presented a plan whereby the owners of the two old papers received stock in a new corporation, the Advocate Publishing Company, in proportion to the assessed valuation of their respective properties. The commission chose for the site of the new enterprise the town of Greensboro, which lay about as far west of the conference dividing line as Durham, the home of Trinity, lay east.[59] On March 14, 1894, the last issue of the "Old Raleigh" appeared. The *North Carolina Christian Advocate* put out its first issue two weeks later. It was edited jointly by the Reverend Mr. Atkins, representing the western conference, and by the Reverend Mr. Grissom of the eastern conference. The two principal stockholders were Grissom and the Reverend Mr. Groome, who had edited the *Western Christian Advocate*.[60] Groome officially replaced Atkins as western editor in January 1895, although he had regularly contributed editorials to the paper over his initials during 1894.

North Carolina Methodists hailed the new enterprise as signaling an end to the denomination's internal strife.[61] But soon the *North*

---

[56]Porter, pp. 60, 86, 87-88; Reidsville *Webster's Weekly*, June 4, 1896; *North Carolina Christian Advocate*, June 28, 1898.

[57]*North Carolina Christian Advocate*, Nov. 4, 1896; *Minutes of the Western North Carolina Annual Conference . . . 1893*, p. 60.

[58]*Journal of the North Carolina Annual Conference . . . 1894*, p. 60.

[59]Raleigh *Christian Advocate*, Jan. 3, Feb. 28, 1894.

[60]On the paper's ownership, see ms. address (1896) in the Grissom Papers; Reidsville *Webster's Weekly*, June 7, 1895.

[61]Raleigh *Christian Advocate*, Feb. 28, 1894; *North Carolina Christian Advocate*, Apr. 4, Sept. 26, 1894.

Carolina Christian Advocate became itself "an agency for division."[62] In the first place, there were conflicts between the owners of the publishing company and the controlling conferences which took some time to straighten out.[63] But the newspaper war also reflected persistent sectional animosities and the disruptive impact of Kilgo's policies. Grissom, as eastern editor, generally followed the Trinity line. Groome, on the other hand, maintained at best a formally correct relationship with the college. Moreover, Groome's advocacy of populistic social reform angered the probusiness Methodist establishment led by Kilgo. On July 15, 1896, without warning, an announcement appeared in the *Advocate* stating that Groome had retired as western editor and sold his interest in the paper to the Reverend L. W. Crawford. Why he did so was unstated but obvious. At the western conference in December 1895, delegates had expressed "some difference of opinion" about the editor's policy. The Trinity trustees were "not satisfied" with his lukewarm support of the college, and some Methodists were appalled at his "criticism of the bankers on the money question."[64]

The policy of the new western editor, however, gave little comfort to the Trinity administration, for he continued to voice the hostility of many of his constituents toward the college. "It's amusing to see how Dr. Crawford compliments you in his editorial scribblings," Professor Mims wrote to Kilgo. "Which one do you love better—Dr. Groome or Dr. Crawford?"[65] On the other hand, Thomas Neal Ivey, who succeeded Grissom as eastern editor in December, advanced his predecessor's pro-Kilgo partisanship. Tarheels referred without exaggeration to the *Advocate* under Crawford and Ivey as a "double-barrel affair."[66] Ivey used the first page of the paper for his editorials, while Crawford wrote his on the eighth page. In addition, the western editor opened the columns of his section to anti-Kilgo articles and letters. This peculiar situation made the *Advocate* quite unusual among southern denominational

[62]M. T. Plyer, "Thomas Neal Ivey: Teacher, Preacher, Editor, Gentleman," *Methodist Quarterly Review* 72 (1923): 679.

[63]Raleigh *News and Observer*, Dec. 15, 1896; *Journal of the North Carolina Annual Conference . . . 1896*, pp. 19, 69-70; ms. address (1896) in the Grissom Papers.

[64]Raleigh *News and Observer*, Dec. 1, 1895.

[65]Mims to Kilgo, Aug. 3, 1896, Trinity College Papers.

[66]Plyer, p. 679.

newspapers, which traditionally did their utmost to gloss over intradenominational quarreling.

By 1896 the state aid issue in North Carolina Methodism had become intertwined with problems arising from the newspaper war, western resentment, hostility to Trinity's policies, and class grievances. This association of issues made Kilgo's opposition to the university appear even more to be not an attack on an elitist institution but a betrayal of the people's welfare. The Reverend R. S. Webb, a westerner, had warned Kilgo upon his arrival in North Carolina against joining the Baptist crusade. Quickly losing confidence in Trinity's new president, he took issue with Kilgo's characterization of free state scholarships as "socialistic" and argued that education required "the best efforts" of church and state. Both needed to respond to the cries of "sorrow and poverty." "Shall the poor be made to feel that the church is their enemy?" asked Webb, echoing Populist complaints. A heated exchange between Webb and Kilgo, the "poor boy" controversy, filled the pages of the Methodist press for almost two months.[67] "It is all nonsense," Crawford said in his western editorial column, "talking about its being better to grow up in ignorance than to be educated in any other than a state school."[68]

Trinity's connection with the Dukes of the American Tobacco Company was galling to some Methodists. A complaint to Kilgo by one Randolph County minister combined a populistic fear of the tobacco trust with a traditional Methodist concern about personal morality:

Trinity was literally a poor man's college. Moving it away from here and planting it in Durham, in the midst of drinking saloons, gambling dens and houses of ill fame, stabbed the church in its vital point, and damaged Christian Education in the State, as it never had been done before. Then putting it in the clutches of the Tobacco Trust Company alienated it from the heart of the people. That Trust Co. has laid its hand on the interests of the farmers of the State and reduced thousands of them to abject poverty. . . . You have only reaped in return the disapproval and detestation of this section of the country.[69]

[67]R. S. Webb to Kilgo, Aug. 2, 1894, Kilgo Papers; *North Carolina Christian Advocate,* July 8-Aug. 26, 1896; *Christian Educator* 1 (Sept. 1896).

[68]*North Carolina Christian Advocate,* July 8, 1896.

[69]L. Johnson to Kilgo, May 1896, Trinity College Papers.

On the other hand, Trinity's most progressive faculty members, including Mims and Bassett, had little patience for such problems and firmly backed their president in the state aid struggle.[70] Moreover, personal morality was a two-edged sword that could be used against Chapel Hill as well as Durham. The university, charged Grissom, tolerated "insubordination, gambling, drunkenness, etc."[71]

The state aid debates at the two Methodist conferences meeting late in 1896 gave some indication of the difficulties Kilgo was encountering, particularly in the West. At the eastern conference he introduced resolutions (which he first had to "tone down" at the request of "conservative men") committing the body "uncompromisingly" to Christian education.[72] The resolutions demanded the abolition of free tuition and scholarships at the university and agreed to appropriations only to meet "the deficiency in current expenses."[73] About two-fifths of the conference "hotly opposed" these sentiments, and the debate on the floor was most unbrotherly. Most of the laymen present, including both Daniels and Cyrus Thompson, were in the opposition.[74] The resolutions had a sufficient majority to pass, but, considering the divisiveness that they engendered, Daniels's *News and Observer* deemed their passage a "barren victory" for Kilgo. "But still," the paper observed two days later, "the adoption of the resolutions puts approval on the idea that the church has the right to make itself heard, as a conference, upon questions that do not enter in the purview of the church."[75]

Apparently most members of the western conference agreed with Daniels, for it chose to reject Kilgo's set of resolutions by a vote of eighty-four to fifty-four. "Most of the laymen and a number of the preachers," according to the *News and Observer*, "are against any action by the conference." The westerners simply endorsed

---

[70]Edwin Mims to Kilgo, Aug. 3, 1896, ibid.; John Spencer Bassett in the *North Carolina Christian Advocate*, Apr. 21, 1897.

[71]*North Carolina Christian Advocate*, Feb. 19, 1896.

[72]Reidsville *Webster's Weekly*, Aug. 5, 1897.

[73]*Journal of the North Carolina Annual Conference . . . 1896*, pp. 14-15.

[74]Raleigh *News and Observer*, Dec. 15, 1896; Robert L. Flowers to [?], Nov. 1896, Trinity College Papers.

[75]Dec. 13, Dec. 15, 1896.

Christian education in very general terms.[76] The reasons for Kilgo's defeat seemed clear to the *Christian Educator:* his opponents were "drag[ging] the methods of politics into our Church Conventions."[77] Yet the division was more fundamental. When the eastern conference declared a year later that "the same trumpet which pressed the lips of Wesley, Coke, and Asbury" had now passed to John C. Kilgo, the western conference chose to denounce the "manufacture, sale and use of cigarettes."[78]

[76]Nov. 22, Nov. 24, 1896; *Minutes of the Western North Carolina Annual Conference . . . 1896,* pp. 30-31.

[77]1 (Dec. 1896): 1.

[78]*Journal of the North Carolina Annual Conference . . . 1897,* p. 46; *Minutes of the Western North Carolina Annual Conference . . . 1897,* p. 19.

V

From War on the University
to a Crusade for Public Schools

METHODIST DISSENSION did not prevent President Kilgo from consummating an informal alliance with the Baptists in the election year of 1896. Columbus Durham, the indomitable secretary of the Baptist state convention, had died in the meantime. The new secretary, the Reverend John Ellington White, while an active opponent of state aid, was a more temperate and circumspect person than his predecessor.[1] Josiah W. Bailey, the editor of the *Biblical Recorder,* had taken second place to Durham two years before but was now the real leader of the Baptist drive. Bailey and White had the advantage of a more united denomination than Kilgo's. The Baptist convention's resolution of 1896, which declared appropriations to the university to be "wrong, unjust and unwise," passed with only two dissenting votes.[2] The *Biblical Recorder,* unlike the Methodist newspaper, was no "double-barrel affair." Although the *Recorder* was the official organ of North Carolina Baptists, Bailey made it into a vigorous advocate of his own political and social views. According to Edwin Mims, the *Biblical Recorder* "rose distinctly above the particular function" it was supposed to serve. "J. W. Bailey did not confine himself to religious subjects that would naturally have appealed to the Baptist denomination, but wrote in a brilliant style of all the questions that were in the public mind." In answer to charges that the *Recorder* was venturing outside its traditional sphere, Bailey wrote, "It is also as really the function of a religious paper to comment upon, to explain, to oppose and disapprove actions and movements of a so-called secular nature, as it is to comment upon matters purely religious."[3] Bailey

[1] For a sketch of White's background, see the *Biblical Recorder,* Dec. 11, 1895. See also Josephus Daniels, *Editor in Politics* (Chapel Hill, 1941), pp. 318-19.

[2] Raleigh *News and Observer,* Nov. 17, 1896.

[3] Mims, "A Semi-Centennial Survey of North Carolina's Intellectual Progress," *North Carolina Historical Review* 24 (1947): 248; *Biblical Recorder,* Feb. 16, 1898. See also ibid:, Aug. 12, 1896.

thus joined Kilgo in rejecting the doctrine of the spiritual nature of the church.

Unlike Kilgo, Bailey began his career by expressing some sympathy for the kinds of reforms Populists were advocating. The *Recorder* vacillated somewhat on the silver question, at times seeming to favor unlimited coinage and at other times downplaying the significance of the issue.[4] Finally by the middle of 1896 Bailey reluctantly came to the conclusion that free silver, although not the answer to all economic problems, would materially benefit the "debtor class" of farmers.[5] He also favored some governmental regulation of railroads and corporations. He urged that the state railroad commission be given increased authority on the grounds that the government ought "to interfere in behalf of its millions of resourceless members, not only for their sake but for the general good." He endorsed popular election of United States senators and government ownership of the telephone and telegraph. The horrors of child labor elicited some of the *Recorder's* most moving editorials. "We believe in the industrial development of our State," Bailey argued. "But we want nothing at the cost of the emasculation of our women and children."[6]

Gradually Bailey modified some of his reformist views. Although he never lost interest in certain problems, such as child labor, he began to share Kilgo's vision of a New South regenerated by corporate capital. In 1894 and 1895 *Recorder* editorials denouncing the American Tobacco Company matched any in the state in their uncompromising hostility. Bailey noted that North Carolina had "suffered more than any other state from [the trust's] power," and he even condemned colleges for accepting endowments from "ill got gains."[7] But the *Recorder* discontinued all attacks on the tobacco trust in 1896, the year in which Bailey and Kilgo began working closely together. By 1898 it contained nothing but praise for the Dukes' "beautiful, holy and blessed" gifts to Trinity College.[8] Following a visit to Trinity in 1899, Bailey wrote to Kilgo,

[4]See, for example, Mar. 7, Apr. 11, 1894, Feb. 5, May 6, 1896.

[5]July 15, 1896.

[6]Feb. 18, 1895, Apr. 22, Sept. 23, 1896, Feb. 15, 1899. See also Aug. 19, Dec. 16, 1896, May 12, 1897.

[7]May 16, 1894. See also Feb. 6, Apr. 24, 1895.

[8]June 15, 1898. See also Aug. 31, 1898.

"Ben Duke reached my heart." By the end of the decade Bailey's effusions were hardly distinguishable from those of other New South propagandists: "The South is in the morning of a new day. Her mines, her forests, her fields, and her factories have begun to attract the tide of population. . . . The new regime in Cuba and the opening of our Isthmian Canal will enlarge her market. . . . Her industrial life is fast becoming like that of the North." In 1900 he supported American intervention in China so that "doors shall be open to our merchants" and "because we have the responsibilities of power." After his election to the United States Senate many years later, Bailey became a leader of the conservative coalition against the policies of the New Deal.[9]

During the election campaign of 1896 and into the legislative session of 1897 Bailey and Kilgo conducted their crusade "with all the zeal of Richard the Lion-Hearted."[10] Complementing Kilgo's Christian education lectures and the efforts of the *Christian Educator,* Bailey thundered against the state institutions in almost every issue of the *Biblical Recorder.* According to Daniels, the two churchmen encouraged each other in their "denunciations."[11] Or, as one of his western opponents said of the president of Trinity, "the mantle of Dr. Durham has fallen on him."[12] Kilgo effusively praised the "fine work" being done by the Baptists, noting that their "work is telling immensely in building up proper educational sentiment."[13] Bailey, now less inclined to flirt with Populist heresies, printed Kilgo's controversial analysis of the "poor boy" with a strong endorsement of it.[14] Moreover, he took editorial potshots at Groome, Kilgo's populistic antagonist on the *Advocate.* By 1897 a warm friendship between the two denominational leaders had grown out of their common struggle. "We are bound together,"

[9]Bailey to Kilgo, June 14, 1899, Trinity College Papers, Duke Univ. Archives; Bailey, "The Case for the South," *The Forum* 31 (1900): 229-30; *Biblical Recorder,* June 20, 1900; John Robert Moore, *Senator Josiah William Bailey of North Carolina: A Political Biography* (Durham, 1968), pp. 110-76.

[10]Luther L. Gobbel, *Church-State Relationships in Education in North Carolina since 1776* (Durham, 1938), p. 148.

[11]P. 232.

[12]Reidsville *Webster's Weekly,* Aug. 5, 1897.

[13]Quoted in Raleigh *News and Observer,* Nov. 6, 1896.

[14]*Biblical Recorder,* July 15, 1896. See also Charles E. Taylor to Kilgo, July 6, 1896, Trinity College Papers.

Bailey told Kilgo late that year, "and the man who strikes you strikes me; and we must together withstand the sisies, the skunks, the demagogs and conspirators. Ours is a Holy Cause."[15]

The Democrats were worried that agitation of the state aid issue might once again work to their party's disadvantage. "In the campaign of 1894," the *News and Observer* reminded the churches, "there was more or less criticism of some ministers of the gospel on account of their active participation in politics. In some cases the churches were injured and political conditions not improved."[16] But the advocates of Christian education were not to be intimidated. Bailey again urged Baptists to be "sure of the soundness of [the] man you vote for. Pledge him publicly. This is the one way to put our principles into effect."[17] Edwin A. Alderman, who had succeeded George T. Winston as president of the university, sounded out the sentiment of politicians throughout the state and discovered that state aid was a very real issue in some areas. His extensive correspondence provides ample testimony that denominational forces were exceptionally active in local campaigns for the legislature and were prepared to work with anyone, regardless of his party, who might oppose state aid.[18] One candidate informed Alderman of being told that "if I will pledge myself against the university I could be elected easily."[19] But there appeared to be no actual collusion between the churches and the Populists, although many Democrats believed that members of the third party were less sound than themselves on the university and hence more susceptible to denominational blandishments. One prominent Democrat told Alderman that if Populists were elected, "God save the state & the university."[20] On the other hand, one Democratic candidate who was "uncompromisingly opposed to the University" won election, allegedly having "appealed to men on no higher ground than narrow church prejudice."[21]

[15]*Biblical Recorder,* July 22, 1896; Bailey to Kilgo, Nov. 9, 1897, Trinity College Papers.

[16]Apr. 26, 1896.

[17]*Biblical Recorder,* Sept. 30, 1896.

[18]The numerous replies to Alderman's inquiries are in the University of North Carolina Papers, UNC Archives, between the dates of Oct. 16 and Dec. 19, 1896.

[19]James O. Carr to Alderman, Nov. 5, 1896, ibid.

[20]James W. Wilson to Alderman, Oct. 22, 1896, ibid.

[21]J. T. Bivins to Alderman, Dec. 12, 1896, ibid.

The Populist-Republican fusionists repeated their 1894 victory by capturing the legislature and electing their entire slate of candidates for state offices, including the governorship. White boasted that the legislature included one hundred Baptists, and Bailey expressed complete confidence that they would do their duty.[22] The *News and Observer* made dire predictions about the fate of the university at the hands of the legislature, doubting that "the excellent forty-four gentlemen who occupy our party's seats" could protect its appropriations.[23] The paper was no doubt being unduly partisan since it was a fusionist legislature which sustained the university in 1895. Moreover, the success of the denominational campaign in electing or defeating certain candidates would not necessarily be reflected in the votes of the legislature. Several of Alderman's correspondents remarked that what a man said during the campaign was no certain indication of how he would vote after party leaders got hold of him in Raleigh.[24]

Both sides went into action when the legislative session began early in 1897. Bailey made a personal appeal to a legislative committee on behalf of what denominational leaders euphemistically called the "voluntary principle."[25] Kilgo, however, was satisfied to publish an open letter to Tarheel lawmakers in which he denounced state aid as "class legislation."[26] Both men were fond of accusing the university of resorting to lobbying tactics, and the Baptist editor even privately urged President Alderman to give up begging money from the legislature and instead seek a private endowment.[27] But Alderman was not disposed to follow such advice, nor did he hesitate to employ the lobbying tactics that the denominational leaders righteously denounced.[28] In his inaugural address of January 1897 the university president defended the scholarship program

[22]Raleigh *News and Observer*, Nov. 21, 1896; *Biblical Recorder*, Dec. 2, 1896; Daniels, p. 230; A. B. Andrews to Alderman, Nov. 13, 1896, UNC Papers.

[23]Dec. 2, 1896. See also Reidsville *Webster's Weekly*, Nov. 19, 1896.

[24]See, for example, the letters to Alderman from James H. Chadbourn, Oct. 17, 1896, W. T. R. Bell, Oct. 19, 1896, W. E. Murchison, Nov. 6, 1896, H. G. Ewart, Nov. 21, 1896, and C. W. Toms, Nov. 30, 1896, UNC Papers.

[25]Raleigh *News and Observer*, Feb. 20, 1897; *Biblical Recorder*, Feb. 24, 1897.

[26]*Christian Educator* 2 (Jan. 1897): 1.

[27]Bailey to Alderman, Jan. 26, 1897, UNC Papers; *Biblical Recorder*, Dec. 23, 1897; *Christian Educator* 2 (Mar. 1897): 1.

[28]See Alderman's correspondence for 1896 and 1897 in the UNC Papers.

and sought to reassure Populist legislators who might still harbor suspicions of Chapel Hill's "aristocratic" reputation:

Over one-half [of the students] are the sons of farmers. Three-fourths are the sons of poor men to whom their presence here means anxiety and self-denial. Eighty are working their way by honorable labor, from waiting at the table to cutting hair. Forty are here as a result of money earned or borrowed. Forty are aided by loans and nearly nine hundred have received aid from the university in the [form of] loans or scholarships in the past twenty years. . . . Is it a crime for the State, for its own sake to aid such people?[29]

Populists and Republicans had rallied to the support of the university in 1895, and on the face of it there was little reason to suspect that the situation would be different in 1897. Both Marion Butler's *Caucasian* and the Winston *Union Republican,* respectively the leading Populist and Republican newspapers, supported the principle of state aid without reservation. "This is no time for tearing down," the *Caucasian* declared. "Let us build up."[30] Republican leaders such as Thomas Settle, Claudius Dockery, Richmond Pearson, Senator Jeter C. Pritchard, A. E. Holton, and Governor Daniel L. Russell gave assurances to Alderman that their party would stand behind the university.[31] Butler worked diligently for the university president behind the scenes to get doubtful Populists in line.[32] During the campaign William A. Guthrie declared that he would regard "any man as my personal enemy who would attempt to tear down and destroy the venerable institution."[33]

But as the legislature set to work, the Populists were more divided on the issue than they had been two years before. In the

[29]Quoted in Kemp P. Battle, *History of the University of North Carolina,* 2 vols. (Raleigh, 1907-12), 2: 538. Alderman had been serving as president since the late summer of 1896. See also an interview given by Alderman to the Wilmington *Messenger,* reprinted in the Raleigh *News and Observer,* Dec. 27, 1896.

[30]Jan. 7, 1897. See also ibid., Dec. 17, 1896; the Winston *Union Republican,* Dec. 24, 1896.

[31]Settle to Alderman, Oct. 26, 1896, Dockery to Alderman, Nov. 10, 1896, Pearson to Alderman, Nov. 25, 1896 (in which Pritchard's and Holton's support is also indicated), and Russell to J. W. Gore, Dec. 1, 1896, UNC Papers. See also Pearson to the Charlotte *Observer,* reprinted in the Raleigh *News and Observer,* Dec. 23, 1896.

[32]Alderman to Butler, Dec. 17, 1896, Butler Papers, Southern Hist. Coll., UNC Library.

[33]Quoted in the Raleigh *Caucasian,* Aug. 6, 1896.

state senate ten of twenty-four Populists opposed the appropriations, and in the house eighteen of twenty-nine, a significant
majority, did likewise.[34] At least three factors may have influenced
those Populists who voted against state aid. In the first place, the
efforts of Baptists and Methodists in the campaign may have borne
fruit, particularly among loyal members of those denominations.
Second, the emphasis in the whole state aid debate concerned
class as much as religion. Both Bailey and Kilgo had stressed the
view that the university educated the few at the expense of the
many and that while the state was wasting its limited resources on
higher education—which, they claimed, the denominational colleges
could easily furnish—the common schools were languishing for lack
of funds.[35] The *Caucasian* recognized the force of this reasoning
and attempted to counter it by showing that the university was an
essential part of the state's whole public school system.[36] Alderman
also spent much time trying to refute this argument, a strong
weapon in the denominational arsenal. William ("Little Bill") Bryan
of Chatham County, the most vocal Populist opponent of state aid
in the house, condemned the appropriations bill as the most
"diabolical class legislation he ever knew." He declared that "all
professional men here were for this bill; but that he represented
the farmers." Taking his cue from Bailey and Kilgo, Bryan denounced lobbyists for the university who were getting paid $2,500
a year by the state for their efforts.[37] Bailey had been flirting with
populistic notions, and Baptist members of the third party might
easily have resented the elitist Episcopalian and Presbyterian flavor
of the university

A third problem hindering Butler's efforts to keep the Populists
in line was party factionalism. The Populist party was changing as
factional infighting and the struggle for place among the leaders
began to undermine the movement's commitment to social change.

[34]The party affiliation of the legislators has been determined by comparing their
votes on state aid with their votes for U.S. senator. In the balloting for senator Populist
votes for the Republican candidate, Pritchard, were listed separately. For the votes for
senator, see Raleigh *News and Observer,* Jan. 20, 1897; and those on state aid, ibid.,
Feb. 24, Feb. 26, 1897.

[35]See Bailey's statements before the house finance committee in the *Christian Educator* 2 (Mar. 1897): 1.

[36]Dec. 17, 1896.

[37]Raleigh *News and Observer,* Feb. 26, 1897.

This fact led to some curious alliances. In 1897 the party divided over whether to support the reelection of Republican Jeter C. Pritchard to the United States Senate. Two years earlier Populists had voted for him, as part of the fusion arrangements, to succeed to the unexpired term of the late Zebulon Baird Vance. In 1897 the majority of Populists, under Butler's prodding, nominated their own candidate, Cyrus Thompson, ostensibly because of Pritchard's goldbug leanings. However, a minority faction, led by Harry Skinner, gave Pritchard just enough Populist votes to insure his reelection.[38] The resulting split in the party, which also involved animosity arising out of the gubernatorial contest in 1896 and the Bryan campaign of the same year, may have affected the vote for the university's appropriations, at least in the senate. In that body not a single Skinner Populist voted for state aid, whereas all but three majority Populists did so. In the house, on the other hand, the Skinner Populists split evenly.[39]

Several weeks before the state aid vote a *News and Observer* editorial referred to a "deal" whereby Pritchard would support Skinner to succeed Senator Butler in 1901. It quoted a "prominent" politician from the western part of the state who talked vaguely of the relationship of "a certain religio-political machine" to Skinner. "I am told," he went on, "that there are one hundred members of the Legislature of our State [John White's one hundred elected Baptists?] who will not vote for any man whose record in respect to church and state is not satisfactory."[40] Skinner had written Alderman in December of his support for the university, but the letter was dated one day before the alleged deal with Senator Pritchard was consummated.[41]

[38]For the senatorial election, see Daniels, pp. 219-20; Helen G. Edmonds, *The Negro and Fusion Politics in North Carolina, 1894-1901* (Chapel Hill, 1951), pp. 61-62; and the files of the Raleigh *News and Observer* and the Raleigh *Caucasian* for Jan. and Feb. 1897. The Cyrus Thompson Papers, Southern Hist. Coll., UNC Lib., which might have thrown some light on the dispute, contain a curious gap for the period covering the senatorial contest.

[39]Raleigh *News and Observer*, Feb. 24, Feb. 26, 1897.

[40]Ibid., Jan. 5, 1897. See also an undated clipping from the Wilmington *Messenger* enclosed in a letter from Daniel L. Russell to B. N. Duke, [1897], Duke Papers, Duke Univ. Lib.

[41]Harry Skinner to Alderman, Dec. 8, 1896, UNC Papers. A conference between Skinner and Pritchard took place in the Ebbitt House in Washington, D.C., on Dec. 9, 1896 (Raleigh *News and Observer*, Jan. 5, 1897).

Whether or not there was such a deal, it was hardly surprising that Butler's work on behalf of the university resulted in more success among those who adhered to his wing in the party. By 1897 the Populist party had become so faction-ridden that any number of problems having little to do with state aid as such could have influenced the vote. In the final analysis, the Populist split did not obscure the failure of Bailey and Kilgo in the legislature of 1897. Just under half of the Populists joined with all but a handful of Democrats and Republicans to support state aid.[42] The lawmakers even increased the appropriations to the university and the normal college. The repeated vows of Bailey and Kilgo not to desert the cause were beginning to sound rather hollow.[43]

A curious by-product of the struggle over state aid was an intensified interest in the public elementary schools, the common schools, of North Carolina. The sad condition of the state's schools in the mid-1890s was unquestionable. The constitution, drafted during Reconstruction under Radical auspices, required that the state maintain a system of public schools for at least four months of the year, but parsimonious conservative administrations failed to provide the funds even for this constitutional minimum. The constitution itself hindered the development of a respectable educational system by limiting the rate of property taxes, the principal source of school revenue, to 66 2/3 cents per $100 assessed valuation, and successive state legislatures were reluctant to appropriate additional funds or tap other potential sources of taxation.[44] Illiteracy continued to be widespread among both whites and blacks.

Such men as Edwin Alderman, Charles McIver, and Charles B. Aycock, who became Democratic governor in 1901, have generally received most of the praise for promoting the state's educational revival. However, the first serious attempts to overcome the miserable condition of the schools were made during the incumbency of Populist state Superintendent of Public Instruction Charles H.

[42]The vote in the senate was 33 to 10 and in the house, 76 to 26 (ibid., Feb. 24, 26, 1897).

[43]*Christian Educator* 2 (May 1897): 1; and *Biblical Recorder,* Mar. 3, 1897.

[44]Louis R. Harlan, *Separate and Unequal: Public School Campaigns and Racism in the Southern Seaboard States, 1901-1915* (paperback ed., New York, 1968), pp. 46-47; and Oliver H. Orr, Jr., *Charles Brantley Aycock* (Chapel Hill, 1961), p. 301.

Mebane between 1897 and 1901.[45] To their credit the Populists had nominated an educator and not a politician to the post. Before assuming office at the age of thirty-five, Mebane had taught six years in the public schools and four years at Catawba College, his alma mater. Believing that the schools should remain out of politics, he refused to participate in the virulently partisan campaigns of the 1890s.[46] To the members of local school boards he gave similar advice, which a historian sympathetic to the Democratic party has called "a highly patriotic action and one characteristic of his official conduct."[47] Nevertheless, the standard history of public education in North Carolina fails even to mention Mebane's name.[48] The *News and Observer* characteristically dismissed him as a "gold-bug . . . wearing the livery of Populism."[49] The Democrats, who later claimed for themselves most of the credit for the state's educational improvement, subordinated the needs of the public schools during the late 1890s to the exigencies of party politics.

Strong support for the public schools also came from another source, the churches. And it came from the same denominational leaders, working closely with Mebane, who opposed state aid to higher education. As early as 1894 Taylor of Wake Forest had argued in his pamphlet against state aid that North Carolina was too poor to support both a university system and a system of elementary education. The state, he insisted, should put its limited resources to work where they could do the most good, in the public schools.[50] Bailey, White, and Kilgo did not fail to keep the issue of the public schools in the forefront of their campaigns in 1896 and 1897. The *Christian Educator* pointed out that too

---

[45] A work which gives proper emphasis to Mebane's role and is by far the best study of education in the South during this period is Harlan, especially chap. 2, "Seedtime: North Carolina in the Nineties," pp. 45-74. For an example of an interpretation that stresses the role of Alderman and McIver in particular, see Hugh Talmage Lefler and Albert Ray Newsome, *North Carolina: The History of a Southern State* (Chapel Hill, 1963), p. 506.

[46] Raleigh *Caucasian,* Jan. 14, Sept. 2, 1897.

[47] Joseph G. deRoulhac Hamilton, *North Carolina since 1860* (Chicago and New York, 1919), p. 305. See also Joseph P. Caldwell to Charles D. McIver, Mar. 31, 1899, McIver Papers, Lib. of UNC at Greensboro.

[48] Edgar W. Knight, *Public School Education in North Carolina* (Boston, 1916).

[49] Oct. 28, 1896.

[50] Taylor, *How Far Should a State Undertake to Educate? or, A Plea for the Voluntary System in Higher Education* (Raleigh, 1894), p. 21.

much emphasis at the top of the educational pyramid was inimical to democracy. There "was no falser doctrine," it maintained, "than that education works down and hence higher education is of supremest value. . . . Instead . . . the reverse is true, it works upward."[51] Bailey promoted education as a cure for both unemployment and poverty.[52] In an address to a mass rally for public education held on the Trinity campus Kilgo declared: "Christianity has a more vital stake in public schools than the State. It grows out of the love of the people. Christ was one of the masses. . . . We can not develop our schools until we bring the church to support them." The meeting sent the legislature a petition demanding the full constitutional school term in every district.[53] White, as secretary of the Baptist convention, spoke before local Baptist associations and urged them to pass resolutions in favor of public education. Both Baptist and Methodist anti-state-aid memorials to the legislature in 1897 stressed the need to spend every available dollar on the common schools. The Methodists even demanded that the school term be lengthened to eight months.[54]

Dr. Thompson, who became secretary of state in the fusion administration, was, along with other Populists, skeptical of denominational solicitude for the masses.[55] He charged that Kilgo was in reality an opponent of public education. In the fall of 1897 Thompson heard a well-publicized sermon that Kilgo delivered in Raleigh. In it Kilgo lashed out at "calamity howlers," "labor agitators," and "christless education." "I'm tired," he fairly shouted, "of this going up and down the country crying out that this nation is going to the bad. Anybody can criticize. . . . Quit this eternal mourning and crying hard times." The president of Trinity added that he preferred North Carolina with its illiteracy to literate Massachusetts "with her loose morals and catalogue of crime."

[51] 1 (Mar. 1896): 1.   [52] *Biblical Recorder*, May 13, Dec. 2, 1896.

[53] Raleigh *News and Observer*, Dec. 22, 1896.

[54] John Ellington White, "When the Tide Began to Turn for Popular Education in North Carolina, 1890-1900," State Literary and Historical Association of North Carolina, *Proceedings* (1922), no. 1 (1923): 39. For the Baptist memorial, see Raleigh *News and Observer*, Nov. 17, 1896; for the Methodist eastern conference's, see *Journal of the North Carolina Annual Conference . . . 1897*, pp. 14-15. The eastern editor of the *North Carolina Christian Advocate* similarly endorsed improved public schools in the issues of Aug. 21, 1896, Jan. 27, May 19, July 7, 1897.

[55] For views similar to Thompson's, see Raleigh *Caucasian*, Dec. 17, 1896, Jan. 7, 1897.

The next day Thompson analyzed the sermon, which was reported to have become the talk of Raleigh. Kilgo had combined, the doctor asserted, a "plea for monopoly" with a "plea for ignorance." According to the *Caucasian,* Thompson "uncovered Dr. Kilgo and laid him bare to the pitiless gaze of the public."[56] The *Biblical Recorder* came to Kilgo's defense and accused Thompson of trying "to destroy the Church" by first destroying Christian education.[57] The *Christian Educator* denied that Kilgo opposed public education; rather, he believed it should be founded on Christian ideals.[58]

To what extent did Bailey and Kilgo use the public school argument simply as a tactical weapon in their fight against state aid? To the *News and Observer* the answer was easy: the denominations were making a "covert attack upon the University under the seeming advocacy of extension of public schools."[59] Looking back many years later, Daniels was still convinced that Bailey and Kilgo had tried to "sugar-coat their hostility" to state aid "though they never did anything effective for public education."[60] According to *Webster's Weekly,* a Reidsville paper long critical of Kilgo, "the opponents of State aid . . . use the common schools as breastworks behind which to fight the higher schools."[61] Bailey, on the other hand, accused Alderman and McIver of being far more concerned about getting support for their own institutions than for the public schools. "They put the Public Schools last—last of all," complained the *Biblical Recorder.* John Spencer Bassett told Herbert Baxter Adams that in the matter of improving the public schools "Trinity and Wake Forest are doing the work for them."[62]

[56]Kilgo and Thompson, ibid., Oct. 28, 1897. See also Raleigh *News and Observer,* Oct. 19, 1897.

[57]Quoted in *Christian Educator* 2 (Nov. 1897): 5-6.   [58]Ibid.   [59]Feb. 21, 1897.

[60]P. 233. Most historians have accepted Daniels's verdict. See, for example, Harlan, pp. 52-53; Rose Howell Holder, *McIver of North Carolina* (Chapel Hill, 1957), p. 154; and Joseph L. Morrison, *Josephus Daniels Says . . . : An Editor's Political Odyssey from Bryan to Wilson and F. D. R., 1894-1913* (Chapel Hill, 1962), pp. 71-72. An exception is Gobbel, p. 192.

[61]Dec. 3, 1896. See also Edwin A. Alderman to Marion Butler, Dec. 17, 1896, Butler Papers.

[62]*Biblical Recorder,* Mar. 3, 1897; Bassett to Adams, Jan. 16, 1896, *Historical Scholarship in the United States, 1876-1901: As Revealed in the Correspondence of Herbert Baxter Adams,* ed. W. Stull Holt (Baltimore, 1938), p. 243.

At a meeting of the state Literary and Historical Association in 1922, White passionately argued that the denominations had been largely responsible for North Carolina's educational awakening. The growing interest in public schools, White maintained, came as a result of the "seemingly reactionary" agitation against state aid. Baptist associations and district Methodist conferences became "public forums for the people, not for political discussion, but for educational arousement . . . until every section of the State had been affected and the people lined up so far as Baptists and Methodists could properly be organized for such a cause." White claimed that the man credited with implementing the state's educational revival, Governor Charles Brantley Aycock, told him of the crucial importance of the Baptist and Methodist work the night before he died.[63]

Mebane seemed to agree that the state institutions of higher learning were more interested in their own welfare than in anything else. This judgment was probably unnecessarily harsh, but it has been overlooked by those who have given Alderman and McIver sole credit for arousing interest in educational reform. "Every public school in North Carolina," the superintendent told Tarheel legislators, "is a State institution. We have appropriations for other State institutions; why not for these State institutions."[64] Mebane assured Kilgo that he would "not endorse any system of supervision that will open the way for a 'University Gang' to control the Public School System of North Carolina." In another letter to Kilgo, whom he addressed as "Dear Friend: & Bro," he praised Trinity for having spoken out "more plainly than any college in the State" in favor of public education. In his official biennial report for 1898-1900—by far the most comprehensive made up to that time by a state superintendent—Mebane expressed his gratitude to ministers who "have preached the gospel of education in the

---

[63]Pp. 58-59. White also told Prof. William Kenneth Boyd of Trinity about Aycock's statement (White to Boyd, July 14, 1922, Boyd Papers, Duke Univ. Archives). For a similar view of the denominational role by a Baptist historian who was acquainted with the Baptist leaders, see George W. Paschal, "The Truth as to Public School Advancement in North Carolina," *Wake Forest Student* 47 (1929):31-61.

[64]Quoted in the Raleigh *Caucasian*, Jan. 28, 1897.

pulpit and in the home, and have done much for the cause of education."[65]

A good deal of cooperation between Alderman and McIver, the denominations, and Superintendent Mebane, strained as it was at times, attended the cause of public school legislation in 1897. In January, Mebane asked the legislature, first, to make a direct appropriation of $100,000 with which the state Board of Education could attempt to equalize school terms throughout the state and, second, to require county commissioners to levy school taxes to institute a four-months term before levying taxes for other matters.[66] He and Bailey worked closely together to secure passage of a bill embodying the superintendent's recommendations. The two men appeared together before the house educational committee. McIver, who was also present, proposed that no school district be allowed to take advantage of the appropriation unless it raised an equal amount itself. Bailey immediately endorsed McIver's suggestion. Almost a month later the legislature passed an "act to encourage local taxation for schools" which provided for a local tax election in every school district on August 10. Any district that failed to approve the tax would be required to hold a similar election every two years until the voters made an affirmative decision. The legislature, however, reduced Mebane's suggested appropriation to $50,000.[67]

The truce between the denominational and state aid forces became more or less official at the Teachers' Assembly in Morehead City in June where Bailey, Kilgo, and Thomas Ivey of the *Advocate* all gave addresses.[68] The assembly named Mebane to head a committee for local taxation which included in its membership Bailey,

[65]Mebane to Kilgo, Jan. 4, 1897, Aug. 4, 1898, Trinity College Papers; *Biennial Report of the Superintendent of Public Instruction of North Carolina for the Scholastic Years 1898-'99 and 1899-1900* (Raleigh, 1900), p. 59.

[66]Raleigh *Caucasian,* Jan. 28, 1897.

[67]Raleigh *News and Observer,* Feb. 19, Mar. 10, 1897; Samuel A. Thompson, "The Legislative Development of Public School Support in North Carolina" (Ph.D. diss., University of North Carolina, 1936), pp. 329-41.

[68]Raleigh *News and Observer,* June 22, June 26, 1897. Alderman made the first gesture of conciliation to Bailey a month earlier (Alderman to Bailey, May 25, 1894 [obviously 1897], copy in the UNC Papers).

Daniels, Presidents Alderman, McIver, and Taylor, and Professor
Robert Lee Flowers of Trinity College. Later, a statewide organization with McIver as chairman and Bailey as secretary carried on
an intensive campaign leading up to the vote on August 10. The
correspondence between the president of the normal college and
the Baptist editor revealed not the slightest trace of past bitterness.
Bailey reported that groups of preachers, teachers, and college
professors were canvassing the counties together.[69] The *Biblical
Recorder,* of course, and Ivey in the *Christian Advocate* came out
strongly behind the movement.[70] Bailey told the state's Baptists
that their greatest need was for an educated membership.[71]

The public school advocates met opposition from an unexpected
quarter. "The politicians are afraid of this question," McIver told
Walter Hines Page.[72] In truth Democratic politicians were less
afraid of the issue than intent upon making political capital out of
it at the expense of the fusionists, the black population, and
the public schools. In June, Daniels urged Tarheels to vote "for
schools" in August. "Every township," his paper noted, "that
votes for a tax . . . takes a step forward." But less than two weeks
later the *News and Observer* made an exception for those townships with "incompetent, venal and unworthy partisans" (that is,
non-Democrats) serving as school committeemen.[73] The Raleigh
daily along with most Democratic newspapers followed with a
campaign designed totally to discredit local taxation while at the
same time they claimed to favor it in principle. Their usual tactic
was to charge black control of white schools since many districts,
particularly in the eastern part of the state, had some black school
committeemen, though usually not more than one in a district.
The Fayetteville *Observer* pointed out that the Cumberland County
school committee contained "a negro man—no doubt a very
worthey man of his race, but still a negro man" who had "control"

[69]Raleigh *Caucasian,* July 1, 1897; White, p. 40; Bailey to McIver, July 19, 1897,
McIver Papers. See also Bailey to McIver, July 13, July 18, 1897, ibid.

[70]*Biblical Recorder,* May 26, June 16, July 14, July 21, 1897; *North Carolina
Christian Advocate,* May 19, July 7, 1897.

[71]*Biblical Recorder,* June 16, 1897.

[72]McIver to Page, July 22, 1897, Page Papers, Houghton Lib., Harvard Univ.

[73]Raleigh *News and Observer,* June 22, July 2, 1897. In a letter to his old and disappointed friend McIver, Daniels admitted his political motives (Daniels to McIver, July
29, 1897, McIver Papers).

over school teachers and children, "female as well as male."[74] The *News and Observer* made a practice of listing districts where blacks exercised "control" of the schools.[75] "It is better," the paper argued, "to tear down the public schools than to permit negro officers to have a voice in the selection of white teachers for white schools."[76] The Wilmington *Messenger* called the local tax "the work of radical and populist legislation" which would lead to "mixed schools."[77] The Charlotte *Observer,* one of the few Democratic papers supporting local taxation, noted regretfully that the friends of the schools had to fight "a good deal of prejudice."[78]

In vain did Bailey remind his fellow Baptists that they "should not let the cry of 'high taxes' or of the 'negro' or of 'politics' prevent them for working every day . . . to carry the election 'For Schools.'" On August 10 only eleven townships voted in favor of the tax.[79] Praising the "heroic work" of Bailey, Alderman, and McIver, Mebane lamented, "It is a sad state of affairs when men will sacrifice the future manhood and womanhood of our poor boys and girls for political purposes."[80] The Democrats had reason to be optimistic. The ineffectiveness of the unqualified support given by Populists and Republicans to local taxation portended trouble for the fusionists in 1898.[81] Although Bailey was "repeatedly told" in 1897 that his advocacy of public schools was "ruining" the Democratic party, it was that party which, in effect, triumphed. In fact, as the Baptist editor confided to McIver, "The Eastern Brethren want to 'Excommunicate' me."[82]

The "Eastern Brethren" came from that part of the state where the black population was largely concentrated—where charges of

---

[74]Quoted in Raleigh *News and Observer,* July 14, 1897. The *News and Observer* reprinted editorials from numerous Democratic newspapers opposing local taxation.

[75]See, for example, July 15, July 17, 1897.

[76]July 28, 1897.

[77]July 21, 1897. See also Aug. 6, 1897.

[78]Aug. 7, 1897. See also Reidsville *Webster's Weekly,* July 27, 1897.

[79]*Biblical Recorder,* July 21, Aug. 18, 1897; Thompson, p. 337.

[80]Quoted in Raleigh *Caucasian,* Aug. 26, 1897.

[81]For fusionist support of local taxation, see ibid., July 1, 1897; interview with Marion Butler in the Raleigh *News and Observer,* Aug. 8, 1897; Winston *Union Republican,* July 22, 1897. A series of editorial postmortems denouncing Democratic tactics appeared in the *Caucasian,* Aug. 12, Aug. 19, Sept. 16, 1897.

[82]Paschal, p. 51; Bailey to McIver, July 19, 1897, McIver Papers.

"Negro rule" made their greatest impact on white voters. It was the Democrats' exploitation of the race issue that, probably more than anything else, defeated local taxation. Democrats could now assume high moral ground and look ahead to 1898 with renewed confidence. "The results [of the vote]," declared the *News and Observer* triumphantly, "teaches that there is no hope for improvement in our educational system until the people drive out the crowd that now profane the temple, and commit the schools and the other affairs of the State to the hands of the intelligence, virtue and patriotism of the State."[83] The Raleigh paper's use of biblical imagery may have been merely rhetorical, but it reflected the unimpaired assumption of men like Daniels that the Democratic party was the proper guardian of the temple and that churchmen who disagreed were at best deluded and at worse perverse. His optimism seemed well-founded. Those who had asserted a new political independence for the churches in their campaigns against state aid and for local taxation now appeared isolated. Perhaps Bailey himself was having second thoughts, for by the end of August he too was following Democratic illogic by blaming the Populists for the defeat of local taxation.[84]

[83]Aug. 12, 1897.

[84]*Biblical Recorder,* quoted in Raleigh *News and Observer,* Sept. 1, 1897.

VI

The Struggle for Power
in Church and Party

JOSEPHUS DANIELS'S characterization of the Democracy as the party of "intelligence, virtue and patriotism" obscured a potentially disruptive factionalism. The resolution of the party's factional conflicts, to a large extent ideological, could have much to do with its chances for victory in 1898 and the course of the state's future development. After two successive state aid defeats and the failure to secure a favorable outcome of the local taxation election, it may have seemed easy to discount any further political role for Bailey, Kilgo, and their supporters. But the state aid fight had obscured larger ideological questions that concerned Bailey and Kilgo. Democratic factionalism had its counterpart in the churches, especially among Methodists. The possibility existed of new kinds of alliances between churchmen and other powerful groups, alliances that Daniels perhaps did not anticipate. A struggle for power was going on in the state, and it involved the denominations as much as the political parties.

The North Carolina Democracy emerged from Reconstruction as a coalition of diverse elements: antebellum Whigs and Democrats, unionists and secessionists, and representatives of the old planter elite and a growing business class. The generally conservative leaders of the party, whom Walter Hines Page excoriated as "mummies," had been unable to cope with increasing popular discontent and had fallen before the onslaught of fusion in 1894.[1] Since the late 1880s certain men had hoped to lead the Democratic party in a new direction. The Farmers' Alliance, for example, first attempted to work within the Democracy to effect reform. When these efforts proved less than successful, many

---

[1]For Page's "mummy" articles, see Burton J. Hendrick, *The Training of an American: The Earlier Life and Letters of Walter Hines Page* (Boston and New York, 1928), pp. 155-92. See also Joseph Flake Steelman, "The Progressive Era in North Carolina, 1884-1917" (Ph.D. diss., University of North Carolina, 1955), pp. 1-56; Otto H. Olsen, "Reconsidering the Scalawags," *Civil War History* 12 (1966): 308-14.

people deserted the old party and joined the Populists.[2] There were other individuals, notably Daniels, who remained loyal to the Democracy but believed that the party, if it was to regain power, had to accommodate Populist grievances. Daniels's true political convictions are difficult to assess since he was first and foremost a practitioner of politics as the art of the possible. Democratic victory was his main concern; and although he never sought elective office himself, he relished the role of political manipulator and, through the *News and Observer,* chief propagandist of his party's cause in North Carolina.[3] He often disagreed with other party leaders, but once they had decided upon a course of action, he loyally went along.

Combining both conviction and expediency, the *News and Observer* enthusiastically supported free silver, filled its pages with antirailroad rhetoric, and became an ardent backer of William Jennings Bryan. In addition, Daniels worked to wean the Populists away from their alliance with the Republicans and to convince the Democrats to enter into fusion arrangements with the third party. In 1896 the simultaneous nomination of Bryan by the Populists and the Democrats permitted electoral fusion for national offices in North Carolina.[4] Early in the same year Daniels cautiously broached the idea of cooperation between Democrats and Populists on the state level, but nothing came of his proposal.[5] Two years later he made a final effort along the same lines. When, at Marion Butler's prodding, the Populist state convention in May made a formal offer to the Democrats for cooperation on all state offices, Daniels vigorously urged that his party, meeting a few days later, accept.[6] Although the Wake County Democratic convention

[2] Stuart Noblin, *Leonidas Lafayette Polk, Agrarian Crusader* (Chapel Hill, 1949), pp. 229-53, 268-95.

[3] Daniels revealed aspects of his political personality in a remarkable letter to Charles D. McIver, Feb. 14, 1894, McIver Papers, Lib. of UNC at Greensboro. For a scholarly defense of Daniels's commitment to progressive reform, see Joseph L. Morrison, *Josephus Daniels Says . . . : An Editor's Political Odyssey from Bryan to Wilson and F.D.R., 1894-1913* (Chapel Hill, 1962), especially pp. 148-86.

[4] Daniels, *Editor in Politics* (Chapel Hill, 1941), pp. 178-79. See also Robert F. Durden, *The Climax of Populism: The Election of 1896* (Lexington, Ky., 1965), pp. 53-54.

[5] Raleigh *News and Observer,* Mar. 1, 1896. See also ibid., Apr. 19, 1896.

[6] Ibid., May 19, May 21, May 27, 1898. The Raleigh *Caucasian* (Mar. 10, Mar. 17, Mar. 24, 1898) reprinted editorials from twelve Democratic newspapers favoring cooperation and twenty-three opposing.

voted almost unanimously to take up the Populist offer, the party's executive committee, dominated by its chairman, Furnifold M. Simmons, and other conservative or business elements, recommended a flat rejection, which the state convention adopted.[7] The New Bern *Journal,* a defender of railroad interests which placed Butler among the "communist leaders [and] the social agitators," praised Simmons as "a straight out Democrat [who] is against every thought or proposition which means fusion with his political enemies."[8] Simmons's own partiality to the big corporations was evident. His law partner and a former Democratic state chairman, James H. Pou, was "counsel extraordinary for all the railroads."[9]

However, Simmons was astute enough to realize that the party would have to make some concessions to Populist sentiment. Hence the platform endorsed such things as free silver, the election of railroad commissioners, and better schools.[10] "It was recognized," according to Daniels, "that the *News and Observer* must be depended upon to influence the Populists to return to the Democratic ranks."[11] But in a move that even such party regulars as Daniels probably did not know about, Simmons and former Governor Thomas Jarvis concluded a secret deal with representatives of "the large corporations." Simmons promised them that in exchange for their support, financial and otherwise, in the campaign the next legislature would not increase taxes or take action hostile to business.[12] After the election E. J. Hale, the editor of the Fayetteville *Observer,* was convinced that such a sellout had

[7] Raleigh *Morning Post,* May 22, May 27, 1898; Raleigh *Caucasian,* June 2, 1898; Raleigh *News and Observer,* May 27, 1898.

[8] June 18, June 3, 1898. See also June 14, Aug. 3, 1898.

[9] Daniels, p. 412. See also W. A. Graham to J. Bryan Grimes, Jan. 11, 1900, Grimes Papers, Southern Hist. Coll., UNC Lib.

[10] Simmons to Matt W. Ransom, Oct. 26, 1898, Ransom Papers, Southern Hist. Coll., UNC Lib.; *North Carolina Democratic Handbook, 1898* (Raleigh, 1898), pp. 188-96. See also Oliver H. Orr, Jr., *Charles Brantley Aycock* (Chapel Hill, 1961), pp. 112, 114-16.

[11] Daniels, p. 244. Daniels characteristically accepted the verdict of his party with regard to cooperation without complaint; see Raleigh *News and Observer,* May 27, 1898. For Democratic skepticism see, for example, Reidsville *Webster's Weekly,* June 2, 1898; Morganton *Farmer's Friend,* Apr. 20, 1898.

[12] *F. M. Simmons, Statesman of the New South: Memoirs and Addresses,* ed. J. Fred Rippy (Durham, 1936), pp. 23, 29. See also Daniels, pp. 320-22, where he claims not to have known of the deal.

occurred and even suspected that "the governing factor" in the rejection of cooperation with the Populists was to secure the state for McKinley in 1900. "Instead, therefore, of a co-operation of Bryanites," he lamented, "we have a fusion of Republicans, Clevelandites and Democrats, all training under the banner of Democracy."[13] The neopopulist wing of the Democratic party was left with little more than rhetoric for comfort.

Conservative Democrats themselves did not form a homogeneous group. Even the label "conservative" is misleading. Many businessmen, including their ideological defenders like Page and Kilgo, saw themselves in the vanguard of progressive change in a backward, underdeveloped South. They had little in common with Page's "mummies" whose real loyalty was to a vanished antebellum arcadia. Among the latter was Theodore Bryant Kingsbury, editor of the Wilmington *Messenger.* Claiming to be a "strict Jeffersonian Democrat," Kingsbury began his long career of opposition to "radicalism" as associate editor during Reconstruction of Josiah Turner's rabid anti-Republican newspaper, the Raleigh *Sentinel.*[14] Later, from the editor's desk of the Wilmington *Morning Star* and then the Wilmington *Messenger,* he continued in his unreconstructed fashion to denounce the subversion of southern traditions. The old man harbored little sympathy for the New South prophets of progress, whom he considered agents of Yankeedom. When, for example, the Reverend Wilbur Fiske Tillett of Vanderbilt in 1887 published an article in a national magazine lauding the virtues of the New South, Kingsbury's response was swift and sure. He detected in Tillett's language "an echo of [George W.] Cable and New England writers." He concluded, perhaps with Henry Grady in mind: "Dinner speeches and postprandial oratory, in which gush and sycophantic adulation are in order, may tolerate the phrase 'New South,' but no genuine son of the South, who is loyal to the past, to his ancestry, to his people, should deliberately employ it." The editor, recalling the "simple grand days of the fathers," reminded his readers that material prosperity, "wealth, luxury and demoralization" do not make a

[13]Hale to Walter Clark, July 4, 1899, *The Papers of Walter Clark,* ed. Aubrey Lee Brooks and Hugh Talmage Lefler, 2 vols. (Chapel Hill, 1948-50), 1: 340-41.

[14]Alfred Moore Waddell to Walter Clark, Nov. 11, 1891, ibid., 1: 247. Biographical details are taken from "Theodore Bryant Kingsbury," in *Biographical History of North Carolina,* ed. Samuel A. Ashe, 8 vols. (Greensboro, 1905-17), 1: 356-62.

great people. A friend, commenting on Kingsbury's tirade against Tillett, thanked him for his "untiring efforts in behalf of Democracy pure and undefiled and true."[15]

New South businessmen, who represented another strain in the Democratic party, also differed among themselves on matters of public policy. Individuals closely aligned with one of the large national corporations operating in the state, such as the Southern Railway or the American Tobacco Company, generally assumed a different attitude toward "trusts" and monopolies than did the regional bourgeoisie—smaller businessmen and capitalists involved in locally owned manufacturing enterprises. Nevertheless, both groups shared a desire not to upset existing social relations and in general to preserve a stable climate for business. They abhorred Populism, and they distrusted Democrats like Daniels who thought that the best way for the party to regain power was to accommodate itself to agrarian discontent. To Robert W. Winston, a Democrat and an attorney closely associated with the Duke interests, Daniels was "thoroughly socialistic"—a notion widely accepted among certain groups.[16]

The two chief vehicles for the business viewpoint were the Raleigh *Morning Post* and the Charlotte *Observer.* When the first issue of the *Morning Post* appeared in December 1897, it was an open secret that the new paper was to have close ties with large corporations operating in the state, specifically the American Tobacco Company and the Southern Railway, whose regional office under the supervision of the line's vice-president, Colonel Alexander Boyd Andrews, was situated in the capital. According to the *News and Observer,* the *Morning Post* was "born in the brain" of Andrews. "Certain gold Democrats . . . gladly subscribed to blocks of stock to organize a paper to stand for 'straight Democracy.' It is even said that a big owner in the Cigarette Trust,

---

[15]Tillett, "The White Man and the New South," *Century Magazine* 33 (1887): 771-73; Wilmington *Morning Star,* Mar. 6, 1897; J. G. Aston [?] to Kinsbury, June 24, 1887, Kingsbury Papers, Southern Hist. Coll., UNC Lib. For a critical view of Kingsbury's hostility to the New South, see Robert Bingham to Walter Hines Page, Dec. 3, 1887 [?], Page Papers, Houghton Lib., Harvard Univ.

[16]Robert W. Winston, *It's a Far Cry* (New York, 1937), p. 218. For a similar view, see Thomas H. Battle to Henry Groves Connor, Mar. 13, 1897, Connor Papers, Southern Hist. Coll., UNC Lib.

a life-long Republican . . . , was so anxious for a 'straight Democratic' paper that he also subscribed for a block of stock."[17] The *Morning Post* did indeed declare its devotion to "straight Democracy," which meant a Democracy uncontaminated by any populistic notions. It never denied charges that Andrews and one or more of the Dukes held a financial interest in the paper. Furthermore, it denounced "hostility to corporations" as "short-sighted" and opposed any attempt at state regulation of railroads. The *Post* stood steadfastly against any form of cooperation with the Populists, who, it claimed, threatened the "business interests and great property rights of North Carolina and North Carolinians." Not surprisingly, the *Post* was an early and enthusiastic backer of Simmons for a seat in the United States Senate and ridiculed suggestions that Daniels be chosen.[18]

The Charlotte *Observer* promoted the economic and political views of Daniel Augustus Tompkins. He purchased the paper in 1891 and offered a half interest to Joseph P. Caldwell, who became its editor. The *Observer* was the chief goldbug and anti-Bryan Democratic journal in North Carolina in the 1890s. Tompkins was a native southern entrepreneur who was skillful in attracting local capital to promote a wide variety of enterprises in the North Carolina piedmont. Among other things, he manufactured cotton mill and cotton oil processing machinery and constructed textile factories, several of which he served as president. Tompkins was also a prolific writer and eager speechmaker who devoted his talents to the promotion of an aggressive capitalism in the New South. His desire to encourage an indigenous southern capitalism, however, made him and the *Observer* vigorous opponents of the domination of the region's economy by northeastern interests and hence of trusts and monopolies in general.[19] Thus, the *Observer* could quite consistently brand the American Tobacco Company as a "great, soulless, insolent combine [which] ought

[17] Raleigh *News and Observer,* Nov. 3, 1897. Justice Walter Clark told Charles McIver that the *Post* "is largely owned by the Dukes" (Clark to McIver, Sept. 17, 1898, McIver Papers). See also Daniels, pp. 235-37.

[18] Dec. 1, 1897, May 11, May 15, May 23, Nov. 18, 1898.

[19] Howard B. Clay, "Daniel Augustus Tompkins and Industrial Revival in the South," in *Essays in Southern Biography,* ed. Joseph Flake Steelman (Greenville, N.C., 1965), pp. 114-45; Daniels, p. 246; Robert H. Wiebe, *Businessmen and Reform: A Study of the Progressive Movement* (Cambridge, Mass., 1962), pp. 77-78, 119.

to be stifled," denounce the "socialism and anarchism" that the Populist movement had allegedly unleashed, and lecture Democrats about the virtues of a single gold standard before the national convention was held in 1896. Needless to say, the *Observer* lent its weight to those forces opposed to cooperation with the Populists in 1898.[20]

The interaction between Democratic and Methodist factionalism derived largely from President Kilgo's relationship, on both an ideological and personal level, with business and corporate interests in North Carolina. Probusiness Democrats became increasingly cordial toward Kilgo despite the fact that the Dukes, Trinity's patrons, were Republicans and that Kilgo refused to identify himself publicly with any political party.[21] Kilgo opposed "selfish" politics, and political instability was bad for business. In any case, the class interests of North Carolina capitalists often transcended party labels, as the Republican Dukes' stake in the "straight Democratic" *Morning Post* indicated. When Kilgo attacked political demagogues it was quite clear he meant only those whose rhetoric seemed to demand a radical change in the system or to challenge certain vested interests, those whom he called "quack healers of all our ills, national and social . . . [who] mistake their empty purses for love of the people, and judge that slander is truth in its most logical form."[22] Kilgo, then, made an easy identification of freedom with order. Those who promoted dissatisfaction, instability, and class conflict were enemies of liberty.

The most obvious link that Kilgo had with the business community was through the Dukes, but there were others as well. W. R. Odell, a major textile manufacturer in Concord, was Kilgo's chief ally in the troublesome western conference.[23] Lee S. Overman, a former Democratic speaker of the state house of representatives and future United States Senator, was a graduate of

[20]Jan. 19, 1895 (see also July 24, 1897), Sept. 29, 1898, June 6, June 12, June 19, 1896, Apr. 8, Apr. 18, 1898.

[21]*Report of the Proceedings of the Investigation of the Charges Brought by Justice Walter Clark against Dr. John C. Kilgo . . . 1898* (Durham, 1898), p. 51 (hereafter cited as *Report of the [Clark-Kilgo] Investigation*).

[22]Quoted in *Christian Educator* 2 (June 1897): 1.

[23]See, for example, W. R. Odell to Kilgo, Dec. 7, 1898, Trinity College Papers, Duke Univ. Archives.

Trinity and friendly to the Dukes, Odell, and the Southern Railway.[24] Simmons himself, another Trinity alumnus, was a member of the college's board of trustees from 1894 to 1910.[25] Colonel Andrews of the Southern Railway not only was "very much obliged" for Kilgo's "kind words" and offers of support[26] but believed that the president of Trinity was "doing more to uplift North Carolina than any [other] man in it."[27] According to Bailey, Kilgo was the only preacher Andrews ever wanted to hear. "The men of influence . . . ," Robert Lee Flowers told Kilgo, "are with you."[28]

Kilgo learned of the establishment of the *Morning Post* from Joseph Gill Brown, a prominent Raleigh banker, "layman extraordinary" of the Methodist church, and a member of Trinity's board of trustees. "Have you seen our new paper 'The Post'?" Brown asked Kilgo. "I am mailing you a copy of it containing a mention of your sermon Sunday night. Come down and help us dispose of the 'scraps.'" The banker assured his friend that the *Post* would take care of the "*very few* disgruntled and envious fellows who still can't read the signs of the times."[29] Kilgo provided to those interests who spoke through papers like the *Morning Post* just the kind of aid that Populists and neopopulist Democrats feared would insure business domination of the state. The group of clergy and laymen that he had brought together in the state aid fight could become quite an effective means of spreading "the idea and ideal" that Colonel Andrews, for one, found so promising.[30] "In fact," Daniels later recalled, ". . . so determined was he [Kilgo] to keep his church as a militant organization along the policies he had laid down that when the *Morning Post* was established at Raleigh, a number of Methodist preachers

[24]Daniels, p. 420; Lee S. Overman to Kilgo, Feb. 9, 1903, Trinity College Papers.

[25]Paul Neff Garber, *John Carlisle Kilgo, President of Trinity College, 1894-1910* (Durham, 1937), p. 351.

[26]Alexander B. Andrews to Kilgo, Jan. 30, 1898, Trinity College Papers.

[27]Quoted in John E. White to Kilgo, June 8 [1900], ibid.

[28]Josiah W. Bailey to Kilgo, June 9, 1900; Flowers to Kilgo, Aug. 16, 1897, ibid.

[29]Brown to Kilgo, Dec. 7, 1897, ibid. See also Robert M. Furman (the editor of the *Morning Post*) to Kilgo, June 19, 1898, ibid. The characterization of Brown is taken from Josephus Daniels, *Tar Heel Editor* (Chapel Hill, 1939), pp. 271, 279.

[30]John E. White to Kilgo, June 8 [1900], Trinity College Papers.

quit taking the *News and Observer.*" In turn Kilgo received lavish praise from the *Morning Post.*[31]

The association of Kilgo with the Duke interests, as well as his opposition to state aid, at first caused the Charlotte *Observer* to exhibit a certain coolness toward him. By the end of the 1890s, however, both Caldwell and Tompkins recognized that Kilgo's leadership in North Carolina Methodism provided an important safeguard against radical agitation. As early as 1896 the *Observer* found much to commend in Kilgo's remarks during the "poor boy" controversy.[32] Caldwell called Kilgo "the most abused man in the state" because of his unpopular stands.[33] The *Christian Educator,* for its part, praised the Charlotte daily as "an honor to journalism . . . [and] always fair" despite its espousal of state aid.[34] Tompkins and Caldwell soon shared a warm respect for the president of Trinity.[35] Fundamental ideological affinity, it seemed, was more important than differences on particular matters of policy.

Both neopopulist and traditionalist Democrats, on the other hand, found Kilgo's activities anathema and, playing upon divisions within the denomination, sought to dislodge him from his position of influence in the Methodist church. Fearing that the fruits of their party's probable victory in the election of 1898 would fall into the laps of New South businessmen, they hoped to use Methodist opposition to Kilgo to forestall this possibility—in effect, to prevent the church from playing a hegemonic role in a business-dominated regime. For traditionalists it was not only Populism that posed a threat but also the aggressive, nationalist New South spirit that Kilgo represented. One Methodist minister even called Kilgo's ideas "radical and revolutionary."[36] Editor Kingsbury of the Wilmington *Messenger* heartily agreed. He was a Methodist "of the old Wesleyan kind," committed to "the simple

[31]Daniels, *Editor in Politics,* p. 119; Raleigh *Morning Post,* June 12, 1898.

[32]June 10, 1896. See also Dec. 9, 1896.

[33]W. B. Harker to Kilgo, July 15, 1897, Trinity College Papers.

[34]2 (May 1897): 1.

[35]See, for example, Caldwell to Kilgo, Dec. 18, 1901, Trinity College Papers; Caldwell to Kilgo, June 16, 1904, Kilgo Papers, Duke Univ. Archives; Kilgo to Tompkins, Dec. 22, 1905, Tompkins Papers, Southern Hist. Coll., UNC Lib.

[36]R. C. Branson to Kilgo, July 23, 1897, Trinity College Papers.

forms and doctrines of the early church"; he had even served in the Methodist ministry from 1860 until 1869. In 1892 he became entangled in a dispute with John Franklin Crowell, Kilgo's prede- cessor at Trinity, who also conceived the college's mission to be the ending of North Carolina's backwardness. Kingsbury de- nounced Crowell as a "Northern man" out of touch with the "manners and customs" of the South.[37]

Kilgo proved no better. In 1897 Kingsbury claimed sarcasti- cally that he was a safer "friend to Trinity College than the gifted president is," after the latter had replied to a *Messenger* editorial claiming that the university had done more for the state "than all the colleges combined." Two months later Kingsbury wrote a lengthy editorial deploring the baneful moral and physical effects of cigarettes and charging the tobacco trust with oppressing the farmers. He also criticized the college for accepting the Dukes' gifts.[38] Kilgo's *Christian Educator* replied in kind, and into the summer the two antagonists hurled charge and countercharge be- tween Wilmington and Durham. When Kingsbury attempted to bring up the old Crowell matter and contemptuously referred to Kilgo as an outsider from South Carolina, the *Christian Educator* reminded him, "This is not a question of yankees and South Caro- linians, and no one need fear that the yankees will again march through the South."[39] Not inconsistently Kingsbury was simul- taneously attacking Walter Hines Page's "Forgotten Man" speech at Greensboro. He accused Page of taking on "Yankee notions" and succumbing to the "ideas and multitudinous 'isms' of New England."[40]

Kilgo's most persistent critic among Democratic editors was John R. Webster. In fact, Kingsbury credited the editor of *Webster's Weekly* of Reidsville with opening his eyes to the true nature of the "vile cigarette tobacco trust" and its relationship to Trinity.[41] Webster's editorials denouncing trusts and railroads

[37]"Theodore Bryant Kingsbury," in *Biographical History of North Carolina*, 1: 356-62; Wilmington *Messenger*, Aug. 5, 1892. See also John F. Crowell, *Personal Recol- lections of Trinity College, North Carolina, 1887-1894* (Durham, 1939), pp. 121-25.

[38]Wilmington *Messenger*, Feb. 2, Apr. 13, 1897.

[39]*Christian Educator* 2 (June 1897): 1; Wilmington *Messenger*, May 30, 1897. See also ibid., July 10, 1897; *Christian Educator* 2 (July 1897): 1.

[40]Wilmington *Messenger*, May 26, May 29, June 8, June 23, June 29, 1897.

[41]Ibid., July 10, 1897.

and calling for the unlimited coinage of silver placed him in the camp of those neopopulist Democrats, like Daniels, who sought to win back rebellious farmers to the old party. Unlike his friend Daniels, Webster had been something of a maverick Democrat and had participated in an antimachine independent movement in the 1880s.[42] Situated as he was in the heart of North Carolina's bright tobacco belt, Webster made the American Tobacco Company the principal object of his editorial wrath. As a loyal Methodist who gave prominent coverage in his paper to local and state denominational affairs, Webster struck hard at the connection between the Dukes and Trinity College. He was probably the first editor in the state to do so. Even before Kilgo's arrival in North Carolina, Webster was denouncing the "abominable cigarette habit" and insisting that "no church or Christian institution could afford to accept blood money from the traffic."[43]

Webster repeatedly urged preachers to take a stand on moral grounds against cigarettes and also against the "godless" trust that produced them. The preachers "are our moral leaders, teachers, and exemplars," he argued. "If they fail to warn the people against evil or condone it in any respect, who can estimate the consequences?" He realized that preachers were not expected to speak out on secular affairs; but since "the trust principle" was "the very antithesis of the gospel," ministers could not remain silent.[44] Against those who would not follow Webster's lead, the *Weekly* lashed out unmercifully. One minister complained of "a mean and bitter attack upon me for my support of Trinity College and the cause of Christian education."[45] Webster accused the trust of trying to buy out North Carolina Methodism by "the occasional flinging of a bone to Trinity College."[46] *Webster's Weekly* carried on a running feud with the *North Carolina Christian Advocate* because of the latter's refusal to attack the trust. Webster condemned the Methodist weekly for having no "backbone."[47] He

[42] Joseph G. deRoulhac Hamilton, *North Carolina since 1860* (Chicago and New York, 1919), p. 215; and Daniels, *Tar Heel Editor,* pp. 339-43.

[43] Reidsville *Webster's Weekly,* July 26, 1894. It is impossible to pinpoint Webster's first attack on the trust or Trinity since only a few scattered issues of the *Weekly* before May 1894 are extant.

[44] Ibid., Dec. 6, 1894. See also July 26, 1895, Sept. 26, 1894.

[45] C. F. Sherrill to B. N. Duke, May 1897, Duke Papers, Duke Univ. Lib.

[46] Reidsville *Webster's Weekly,* Sept. 9, 1895.

[47] Ibid., Oct. 17, 1895. See also Sept. 19, Oct. 24, 1895.

easily made the connection between "Kilgoism and the Trusts"
and advised the president to give himself "the full treatment along
the line of Christian education."[48] In a report on one of Kilgo's
sermons, Webster pictured him as an arrogant and demagogic
preacher:

> Dr. Kilgo impressed us as a man of parts, bright, eloquent and magnetic,
> and if he could keep himself in the background he would be an excellent lec-
> turer. He has a high opinion of Kilgo and just can't hide that fact. . . . It is
> Kilgo that has discovered the inherent depravity of state education; it is Kilgo
> that knows the politicians through and through; it is Kilgo that can put an
> army to flight; it is Kilgo that can run the straightest furrow in North Caro-
> lina. . . .
>
> Dr. Kilgo was severe on whiskey, but had nothing to say about cigarettes.
> He opened the flood gates on the corruption of politics, but was strangely
> silent on the principle source of corruption, the trusts, which spend millions
> to control conventions and corrupt the suffrage.[49]

These attacks on Trinity's president coalesced during the
months before the 1898 election in the so-called Clark-Kilgo affair. Walter Clark was a Democrat who had served on the state
supreme court since 1889. In 1894 he received not only his own
party's nomination for reelection but also the endorsement of the
Populists and Republicans. This action was an acknowledgment of
both his immense popularity with the voters and, at least as far as
the Populist party was concerned, his commitment to social reform.[50] Though the scion of planter aristocrats, Clark was the
most prominent advocate of reformist measures in North Carolina.
On the bench and off, in numerous articles and addresses, he bat-
tled against the "interests" on behalf of the "masses." He worked
assiduously for railroad regulation, government ownership of the
telephone and telegraph, free silver, popular election of senators,
the income tax, postal savings, maximum hours and minimum
wages for labor, child labor legislation, women's suffrage, and the
end of the use of injunctions to break strikes. As a justice, particularly in his 371 dissenting opinions, Clark was one of the most
notable advocates in the country of reform of the court system,

[48]Ibid., Nov. 26, Oct. 17, 1895.

[49]Ibid., Apr. 15, 1897.

[50]Aubrey Lee Brooks, *Walter Clark, Fighting Judge* (Chapel Hill, 1944), pp. 69-71.

favoring the limitation of the power of judicial review and the popular election of judges.[51]

Clark's views were naturally discomforting to Tarheel conservatives, many of whom considered the judge a "socialist" or, in the words of fellow judge Henry Groves Connor, "the most dangerous man in the State."[52] Clark was hardly that. He was an outstanding example of a paternalistic reformer-aristocrat who distrusted big business and sought to direct the Democratic party toward social reform. The feeling of many Democrats that the judge was at least tainted with Populism, particularly after the third party endorsed him in 1894, had no little justification.[53] Clark worked intimately with Marion Butler on reform issues during the 1890s and of course supported Democratic cooperation with the Populists. According to the analysis that Clark made to Butler of the Democratic state convention in 1898, the party would have endorsed cooperation if the silver forces had had "pluck." "Andrews' Attys," he maintained, "were so blatant that they over awed and ran over those who should have stood by Mr. Bryan."[54] The judge himself had experienced the wrath of the railroads. One Democratic politician pointed out that Clark could not get that party's nomination for governor in 1896 because "he could not get railroad backing which amounts to over thirty thousand votes in the democratic party." "The corporations," Clark complained to Butler, "have a tremendous impact in North Carolina politics and legislation."[55]

The judge was an active layman in the Methodist church. Among other things, Clark had been involved in the negotiations leading to the division of the denomination in North Carolina into two conferences, had drafted the plan for the consolidation of the

[51]Ibid., pp. 85-101, 207, 257-65; *Papers of Walter Clark*, 1: 301-2, 307, 308-21, 328-32.

[52]Connor to George Howard, Feb. 9, 1901, copy in the Connor Papers. See also Robert Watson Winston, "North Carolina: A Militant Mediocracy," *Nation* 116 (Feb. 21, 1923): 218. For an appreciation of Clark by a Virginia socialist, see Walter Marion Raymond to Clark, Aug. 27, 1905, Clark Papers, N.C. State Archives.

[53]*Papers of Walter Clark*, 1: 240.

[54]Clark to Marion Butler, May 30, 1898, ibid., 1: 334. Between 1895 and 1899 Clark and Butler exchanged at least twenty-seven letters. See ibid., 1:280-350 passim.

[55]L. F. Telfair to J. Bryan Grimes, Jan. 12, 1896, Grimes Papers; Clark to Butler, Apr. 2, 1898, *Papers of Walter Clark*, 1: 330.

North Carolina Christian Advocate, had served as a lay delegate to several general conferences and to the ecumenical conference of Methodism in London in 1881, and since 1889 had been a trustee of Trinity College.[56] In 1894 John F. Crowell desired "exceedingly" to place Clark's name in nomination as his successor to the presidency of Trinity, but the judge declined the compliment.[57] Clark's religious convictions gave his demands for reform an evangelistic fervor and imparted to his writings and speeches the same sense of moral urgency that animated the social gospel movement. "The central idea of the teachings of Christ," he told a Sunday school conference, "is that between the supremest of the supreme power and the humblest individual the dignity of manhood requires and permits no human intermediate. There you have the great thought of the equality of mankind."[58]

With the failure of Populist-Democratic cooperation, Clark still persisted in his efforts to prevent the domination of state politics by business interests although it was no longer possible to do this by using his party's machinery. However, a controversy that had been simmering for almost a year between him and President Kilgo provided a golden opportunity for demonstrating to the people the extent of corporate subversion of their institutions. Clark's criticism of institutionalized religion agreed with much of what the Populists had been saying about the churches since 1895. In June 1897 Clark declared:"Our people are being robbed by wholesale. They do not receive the just rewards of their labors. They are being pauperized, and kept in want while a few men, by trick and combinations, are gathering to themselves the earnings of a continent. Yet how many leading church members, how many church papers are denouncing the robbers and the wrongs as the Master did . . . ? How many indeed are pursuing an opposite course? . . . Let each man's conscience answer him."[59] One leading churchman seemed to fit exactly the specifications of those whom Clark criticized, and in the same month the judge made his first accusations against the president of Trinity.

[56]Brooks, p. 59; *North Carolina Christian Advocate,* Jan. 3, 1894.

[57]Crowell to Clark, June 8, 1894, *Papers of Walter Clark,* 1: 274; Raleigh *News and Observer,* June 6, 1894.

[58]Clark, "Political Teachings of the Gospel," address before the Raleigh District Sunday School Conference, June 15, 1897, *Papers of Walter Clark,* 1: 463-64.

[59]Ibid., 1: 466.

Clark's concern ostensibly had to do with a proposal of Kilgo's to extend the term of faculty appointments at Trinity from one to four years. A special committee of the college's trustees, chaired by Clark, reported against the president's suggestion. Word got to Kilgo that Clark had based his action on the grounds that the proposal was really a scheme to insure the president's own tenure for at least four more years. A lengthy exchange of letters between the two men ensued. The judge referred to a "growing opposition" to Kilgo "in the tobacco section especially." He frankly told the former circuit rider that he could not last in North Carolina "unless you are protected by a four years' term or some influence not based on public esteem." Moreover, students at Trinity were "proselyted and taught political heresy foreign to the faith of their fathers."[60] On July 15, the day after Clark mailed his last letter to Kilgo, Josiah Bailey was at the judge's house. The next day the Baptist editor warned Kilgo that "beyond a peradventure" Clark "carries a knife under his shirt for you." Kilgo was then engaged in controversy with editor Kingsbury, and under the circumstances Bailey advised his friend "to be as careful as possible . . . [and] guard your utterances."[61]

There the matter rested until the next meeting of the Trinity trustees on June 6, 1898, well into the election year. Kilgo, as he had warned Clark a year earlier he would do, laid their entire correspondence before the board, although the judge was not present. The trustees deprecated Clark's charges and resolved that he "ought to" resign from the board.[62] Some days later Clark wrote to James H. Southgate, the chairman of the board, complaining that he was given "no notice, no chance to put in evidence, nor present an argument." He charged that the proceeding had been instituted "to soothe Dr. Kilgo's vanity and to placate the Trust that more money might be obtained from it." Using as an excuse the appearance of an article on the affair that appeared in the Charlotte *Observer* on June 24, Clark gave the entire correspondence between himself and Kilgo and Southgate, together with a

[60]Clark to Kilgo, July 14, 1897, *Report of the [Clark-Kilgo] Investigation,* pp. 7-8. See ibid., pp. 5-8, for the letters exchanged between Clark and Kilgo. For a spirited defense of Clark's role, see Brooks, pp. 102-21. For an equally emphatic defense of Kilgo, see Garber, pp. 212-29. A more balanced summary is in Earl W. Porter, *Trinity and Duke, 1892-1924: Foundations of Duke University* (Durham, 1964), pp. 79-83.

[61]Bailey to Kilgo, July 16, 1897, Trinity College Papers.

[62]*Report of the [Clark-Kilgo] Investigation,* p. 10.

lengthy interview, to the *News and Observer*.[63] Although the
parties concerned denied releasing the original story to the
Observer, it is clear that Clark desired to bring the matter out into
the open. John Webster, who worked closely with the judge during
this period, indicated as much.[64] Clark had told Southgate that he
intended to submit the matter to the people and would accept
"their verdict—not yours." Next it was Kilgo's turn for a newspaper interview—this time in the *Morning Post.* The president demanded a full-scale investigation of his record by the board of
trustees so that he might clear himself of all charges.[65]

A few days later Clark received notice that the board would
convene on July 18 and would consider five accusations against
Kilgo that Clark had outlined earlier in a letter to Southgate:
Kilgo's evasion of Clark's evidence, his "affluence of sycophancy"
toward Washington Duke, his reputation in South Carolina as "a
wire-puller of the ward politician type" and in Tennessee as "a
scrub politician," and his record in North Carolina.[66] At Clark's
insistence both sides were given until August 30 to collect evidence and secure witnesses. During the next six weeks, as representatives of defense and prosecution scurried to and fro across
both Carolinas obtaining depositions and attempting to round up
generally reluctant witnesses, Clark and Kilgo (usually via hard-
pressed Chairman Southgate) exchanged accusations about the
fairness of the proceedings. Clark, however, had no illusions about
the outcome of the contest. "The jury is packed, the witnesses are
bulldosed," he remarked to his brother-in-law. "I can only do the

[63]Clark to Southgate, June 25, 1898, ibid., pp. 11-13; Raleigh *News and Observer,*
June 26, 1898; Charlotte *Observer,* June 24, 1898. See also Gattis v. Kilgo, 128 N.C.
402.

[64]Charlotte *Observer,* June 27, 1898; Reidsville *Webster's Weekly,* July 7, 1898. On
the close association of Clark and Webster during the controversy, see E. W. Fox to
Kilgo, Aug. 1, Aug. 2, 1898; J. H. Cunninggim to Kilgo, Aug. 3, 1898, Trinity College
Papers; *Suppressions and Omissions in the So-Called "Minutes" of the So-Called "Investigation" of Dr. J. C. Kilgo, by the Board of Trustees of Trinity College, August 30-31,
1898* (n.p., n.d.), p. 8; Gattis v. Kilgo, Granville County [N.C.] Superior Court, January
Term, 1900, p. 140, typescript in Duke Univ. Lib.

[65]Clark to Southgate, June 25, 1898, *Report of the [Clark-Kilgo] Investigation,* p.
13; Raleigh *Morning Post,* July 3, 1898.

[66]Clark to Southgate, June 25, 1898, *Report of the [Clark-Kilgo] Investigation,* p.
13; Southgate to Clark, July 7, 1898, *Papers of Walter Clark,* 1: 393.

best I can trusting the public will grasp the 'true inwardness' of the situation."[67]

The direction of the "trial," which lasted two days, was clear from the beginning, when Clark was unable to get even a second to his motion challenging the competency of certain members of the "jury" to hear the case. Many witnesses who had been called by the prosecution refused to attend from fear of retaliation, according to Clark, by "Dr. Kilgo's faction and the large business interest which is backing him."[68] Even more indicative of the course of the trial was the omission in the final agenda of the charge concerning Kilgo's record in North Carolina. Southgate had included this part of the indictment in his letter to Clark on July 7, and John R. Webster had been officially notified to testify on this point. But the board acceded to Kilgo's demand that his career in North Carolina not be considered, despite Clark's strenuous objection. Accordingly, Southgate ruled Webster's testimony and several depositions collected in North Carolina out of order.[69] In his own defense, Kilgo asserted that Clark's charges had been trumped up as part of a plot to chain Trinity to the "dominant party" in the state. "Such bondage," he inisted, "is the degradation of all thought." He arraigned a certain "political crowd that has sprung up who are determined to enslave every college for their purposes."[70] To no one's surprise, the board of trustees acquitted Kilgo of all charges.

The political implications of the controversy made it a staple item for the North Carolina press. The Reverend Mr. Ivey's condemnation in the *Advocate* of "vituperative" newspaper involvement did little good. Next to the war with Spain, the *Morning*

---

[67]*Report of the [Clark-Kilgo] Investigation*, pp. 23-41; B. C. Beckwith to Southgate, Aug. 11, 1898, Kilgo to Southgate, Aug. 13, 1898, G. A. Oglesby to Clark, Aug. 16, 1898 (copy), and Southgate to Clark, Aug. 19, 1898 (copy), Southgate Papers, Duke Univ. Lib.; Clark to A. W. Graham, Aug. 29, 1898, *Papers of Walter Clark*, 1: 385-86.

[68]*Report of the [Clark-Kilgo] Investigation*, p. 48. See also Raleigh *News and Observer*, Aug. 31, 1898; Clark to A. W. Graham, Aug. 27, 1898, *Papers of Walter Clark*, 1: 385.

[69]*Report of the [Clark-Kilgo] Investigation*, p. 69; *Suppressions and Omissions*, pp. 52-56; *Papers of Walter Clark*, 1: 399-401.

[70]*Report of the [Clark-Kilgo] Investigation*, pp. 156-57.

Post asserted, nothing had excited the public interest more. According to Robert Winston, it split the Methodist church "from center to circumference." Moreover, as Winston saw it, the whole affair "was a fight to the finish—a fight between the radical advocates of William J. Bryan and his policies and the more conservative wing of the Democratic Party—a fight growing out of the fierce campaign of 1896." The *Patron and Gleaner* of Northampton County, a paper friendly to Clark, predicted that the affair would "result in great injury to the Methodist church . . . [by] arraying the college and its rich donors (the Tobacco Trust people) and a majority of the ministers of the church on one side, and the rank and file of the 135,000 Methodists . . . on the other side." "Politics," the paper concluded, "has entered the discussion, in fact has been in it from the first."[71]

At the hearing no representatives of the press were permitted. At the beginning of the proceedings, Professors Bassett and Flowers had to eject forcibly a *News and Observer* correspondent. So great was Kilgo's ire that he jumped up, locked the door, and declared that Daniels's daily was "not a decent paper and was not entitled to circulation into any household that pretended to be decent."[72] The absence of the press posed a problem for Clark, who had prepared his own lengthy statement to the board. The judge chose to relinquish his opportunity to speak after the trustees ruled that he first would have to agree not to make his address public. Then, on September 4, his undelivered remarks appeared in the *News and Observer* and later in other newspapers friendly to his cause, often in special supplements.[73] Four days later, the *Morning Post* followed with the publication of Kilgo's address to the board and called Clark's speech "not fair." "The animus of Judge Clark is personal and political," reasoned the *Post*. "He hates Dr. Kilgo. His letters show it. He is trying to make capital politically."[74] The

[71]*North Carolina Christian Advocate,* July 6, 1898; Raleigh *Morning Post,* July 3, 1898; Winston, "Gattis v. Kilgo," undated ms. in the Winston Papers, Southern Hist. Coll., UNC Lib.; Rich Square *Patron and Gleaner,* July 7, 1898.

[72]Gattis v. Kilgo, Granville County [N.C.] Superior Court, January Term, 1900, pp. 140-41, typescript in Duke Univ. Lib.

[73]Raleigh *News and Observer,* Sept. 4, 1898; Reidsville *Webster's Weekly,* Sept. 8, 1898; Rich Square *Patron and Gleaner,* Sept. 8, 1898; Fayetteville *Observer,* Sept. 8, 1898.

[74]Sept. 8, 1898.

Post had published Kilgo's defense only after he and his friends had tried to pressure the *News and Observer* into not accepting Clark's speech. They sent to Raleigh the Reverend N. M. Jurney, a Trinity trustee, who told Fred Merritt, the reporter who had covered the case, that "it would be better for him personally, better for the *News and Observer* and better for the Democratic party," if Clark's statement remained unpublished.[75] By the end of the month not only were most of the state's newspapers filled with conflicting testimony and opinions on the Clark-Kilgo controversy but the Trinity trustees had also printed and distributed 10,000 copies of an "official" report on the whole affair; and close on their heels Clark's friends brought out the *Suppressions and Omissions in the . . . "Investigation" of Dr. J. C. Kilgo.*[76]

There was a close correlation between the ideological proclivities of a sample of Democratic newspapers and their attitudes toward Clark's challenge to Kilgo. Table 1 indicates that those Democratic newspapers which opposed fusion with the Populists, with one exception, supported Kilgo or remained neutral, whereas those which favored some kind of cooperation with the third party aligned themselves solidly behind the judge. Benjamin R. Lacy, a friend of Clark's and a Democratic politician, explained to Charles McIver the basis for the division in the controversy: "As a very rich successful man told me concerning the Clark-Kilgo broil, '. . . it is simply the two ideas of silver and gold clashing. I am for Kilgo because he represents *us.*'"[77]

The Clark-Kilgo controversy threatened to divide the North Carolina Democracy dangerously in a year that was to be decisive for its future role in the state. Jurney's warning to the *News and Observer* indicated as much. The Reverend E. A. Yates, a Kilgo supporter, told the *Morning Post* that he was a Democrat but added,"party shall not stand in the way of my duty to God and my religion, nor prevent me from standing by truth and right." At least one Methodist Democrat proceeded to read Clark out of the party. "I am a Democrat," he wrote to Kilgo, "but no self-seeking demagogue Populist like Walter Clark is." A preacher told Kilgo that "when any political party hits the Methodist Church . . . ,

[75]*Suppressions and Omissions,* pp. 2-3. See also Clark to A. W. Graham, Sept. 5, 1898, Graham Papers, Southern Hist. Coll., UNC Lib.

[76]Gattis v. Kilgo, 128 N.C. 402. [77]Lacy to McIver, July 6, 1899, McIver Papers.

Table 1. Alignment of Democratic newspapers on fusion and Clark-Kilgo controversy

Newspaper	Fusion	Clark-Kilgo controversy
Statesville *Landmark*	unfavorable	pro-Kilgo
High Point *Enterprise*	unfavorable	pro-Kilgo
Winston *Sentinel*	unfavorable	pro-Clark
Statesville *Mascot*	unfavorable	neutral
Tarboro *Southerner*	unfavorable	neutral
Concord *Standard*	unfavorable	pro-Kilgo
Wilmington *Star*	unfavorable	neutral
New Bern *Daily Journal*	unfavorable	pro-Kilgo
Charlotte *Observer*	unfavorable	neutral
Morganton *Herald*	unfavorable	pro-Kilgo
Raleigh *Morning Post*	unfavorable	pro-Kilgo
Jonesboro *Progress*	favorable	pro-Clark
Raleigh *News and Observer*	favorable	pro-Clark
Rich Square *Patron and Gleaner*	favorable	Pro-Clark
Fayetteville *Observer*	favorable	pro-Clark
Reidsville *Webster's Weekly*	favorable	pro-Clark
Morganton *Farmer's Friend*	favorable	pro-Clark

Sources: See the Raleigh *Caucasian,* Mar. 10, Mar. 17, Mar. 24, 1898, for the attitudes toward fusion of the Statesville *Landmark,* Winston *Sentinel,* and Jonesboro *Progress.* See the Raleigh *Progressive Farmer,* July 12, 1898, for the attitudes toward Clark and Kilgo of the Statesville *Landmark,* High Point *Enterprise,* and Winston *Sentinel.* See the Reidsville *Webster's Weekly,* July 7, 1898, for the attitude of the Jonesboro *Progress* toward Clark and Kilgo. For the following newspapers, the first date indicates attitude toward fusion, and the second, that toward Clark-Kilgo (one date means no mention of Clark-Kilgo): Statesville *Mascot,* June 2, 1898; Tarboro *Southerner,* May 19, Aug. 4, 1898; Concord *Standard,* May 21, July 1, 1898; Wilmington *Star,* May 20, 1898; New Bern *Daily Journal,* May 19, July 2, 1898; Charlotte *Observer,* Apr. 18, June 27, 1898; Morganton *Herald,* June 2, Sept. 15, 1898; Raleigh *Morning Post,* May 23, June 30, 1898; Raleigh *News and Observer,* Apr. 12, Sept. 4, 1898; Rich Square *Patron and Gleaner,* May 26, July 7, 1898; Fayetteville *Observer,* May 20, Sept. 8, 1898; Reidsville *Webster's Weekly,* Apr. 14, July 7, 1898; Morganton *Farmer's Friend,* Apr. 20, July 6, 1898. No mention of Clark-Kilgo is taken to mean neutrality.

then I am *agin* that Party." Key party organs like the pro-Clark *News and Observer* came under heavy Methodist fire. Ivey, for example, declared in the *Advocate* that such newspapers were "governed by motives, malignant, mercenary or political."[78]

The business wing of the Democratic party remained almost solidly in Kilgo's camp. Webster's charge that every Trinity professor save one had voted for McKinley in 1896 seemed to make little difference to the "straight Democracy."[79] The Dukes and the chief counsel for the American Tobacco Company, W. W. Fuller (who had been active in Democratic politics in North Carolina before moving to New York), took a personal interest in the controversy; and all worked closely with the Raleigh *Morning Post* in mapping Kilgo's strategy. Fuller wrote Southgate of his approval of the *Post's* editorial policy, and he urged Ben Duke to advise Kilgo to "cut to the bone, but with a sharp knife." Fuller also suggested that Colonel Andrews "might be of some help."[80] Robert Furman, the editor of the *Morning Post,* offered and sought advice on the best way to defeat the judge.[81] Fabius Busbee, a Southern Railway attorney and promoter of the line's interest within the Democratic organization, assured Ben Duke that although he had opposed the war on the university, he was with Kilgo all the way in his fight with Clark.[82] The New Bern *Daily Journal,* a defender of railroads published in Chairman Simmons's home town, denounced Clark's action as "sinister" and branded the judge a "talented but unscrupulous demagogue."[83] The position of these

[78]Yates to the Raleigh *Morning Post,* n.d., clipping in the Kilgo Papers; C. N. Williams to [Kilgo], n.d., L. J. Holden to Kilgo, Aug. 22, 1898, Trinity College Papers; *North Carolina Christian Advocate,* Sept. 21, 1898.

[79]Reidsville *Webster's Weekly,* July 28, 1898.

[80]W. W. Fuller to Southgate, July 2, 1898, Trinity College Papers; Fuller to B. N. Duke, June 29, 1898, Duke Papers. See also Joseph G. Brown to Duke, July 11, 1898, ibid.

[81]For example, Furman wrote to Southgate: "You have read Judge Clark's article in News-Observer this A.M. He sent it to Post also. . . . I will insert it in the morning and put Dr. K's interview in Sunday's issue. His reply is, as you see, along the lines I suggested it would be, and [I] think Dr. K's *covers the points.* . . . If you and Dr. K. think there is anything in the last article not covered by the reply of the Dr., write out your thoughts thereon and send me tomorrow. . . . I think he [Clark] will be willing to quit after this" (July 1, 1898, Trinity College Papers; see also Furman to Kilgo, June 19, 1898, ibid.).

[82]Busbee to Duke, July 2, 1898, ibid. On Busbee's railroad activities, see Daniels, *Editor in Politics,* pp. 157, 410-13; Brooks, p. 133.

[83]June 3, June 14, July 2, July 21, Aug. 3, Sept. 3, 1898.

Democrats and party spokesmen was no doubt of immense benefit to Kilgo personally, and it also indicated a determination to stifle any attempt by men like Clark to change significantly the ideological direction of state politics. It was essential that Trinity College and the leadership of North Carolina Methodism remain a bulwark of stable capitalist development.

Clark and his supporters were troubled about the implications of Kilgo's victory and the considerable support he received from certain groups in the state. The president of the Farmers' Alliance, William A. Graham (recently returned to the Democratic fold), referred in his speeches to Kilgo's denunciations of free silver as an example of the sort of influence his party was supposed to be fighting. Graham was mortified to discover that Simmons had authorized members of the Democratic executive committee to distribute to the voters Kilgo's defense speech before the Trinity trustees. "They sent out the Daily [Morning] Post of the 16th with K's speech as a supplement—as a campaign document—thus lending Andrews the machinery of our party."[84] Kilgo's continued domination of Trinity and the Methodist church seemed to foreshadow what was in store for the state. "The trial is a specimen to the people," Clark observed, "of how they will be tried in the civil courts if the Trusts can get as full control of our civil govt. as they have of Trinity College."[85]

The dispute between Clark and Kilgo provided the Populists with new ammunition for their contention that the churches were subservient to vested interests. Both the *Caucasian* and the *Progressive Farmer* gave wide publicity to the controversy and remained strong partisans of the judge's cause. The Populist handbook for the 1898 campaign accused the "Democratic machine" of tolerating Kilgo's "slanders" while at the same time condemning the atrocities of "Negro rule" during the fusion administration.[86] A *Progressive Farmer* editorial, anonymously penned by Cyrus Thompson, linked the current controversy to the earlier

[84]W. A. Graham to A. W. Graham, Nov. 7, 1898, Graham Papers. See also W. A. Graham to A. W. Graham, Sept. 20, Oct. 17, 1898, ibid.

[85]Clark to A. W. Graham, Sept. 5, 1898, ibid. See also Clark to Graham, Sept. 12, Sept. 20, 1898, ibid.

[86]Raleigh *Caucasian,* June 30, July 7, July 28, Sept. 29, 1898; Raleigh *Progressive Farmer,* July 12, July 26, Aug. 16, Sept. 6, Sept. 27, 1898; *People's Party Hand-Book of Facts, Campaign of 1898* (Raleigh, 1898), p. 88.

Populist critique. It declared: "It is worthwhile to inquire where this money domination will end. Applied already in institutions of learning, to professors, presidents, and trustees, institutions of the Church, why should it not be applied to the Church itself? Then it will be that . . . no gospel will be preached that does not deify the rich and content itself with the giving of Dives-crumbs to the poor. And all this prospect of things comes to view in North Carolina, at least, under the guise of Christian education."[87] Thompson, then, realized that just as the Old Order had exercised its hegemony in part through a social and cultural consensus, of which the church was an important element, the New Order, more closely aligned with the business interests of the New South, could use religion in much the same way. The revolt of the Populists, the attack of some of their leaders on the churches, and the state aid fight had caused a partial breakdown in the relationship of religion to the social order. Clark tried to prevent the forging of new bonds, but ironically, as conservatives and the business community rallied to Kilgo's support, his efforts seemed to have precisely the opposite effect.

Still, Clark hoped that Kilgo's vindication by the trustees would be repudiated by the church. His challenge of Kilgo took into account the considerable opposition that already existed in the Methodist church toward the policies of Trinity's president. Clark no doubt hoped to use the grievances of many rank-and-file Methodists for the purpose of destroying the influence of Kilgo—and his business ideology—within the church and thus preventing its becoming a bastion for those forces he was fighting in the Democratic party.[88] The danger was that many preachers would regard Clark's charges against Kilgo as an attack on their order in general. Thus his whole strategy could easily backfire. Although the judge made a point of assuring the ministers on the Trinity board that in criticizing Kilgo he was not attacking all clergymen, the church, or religion, not all preachers agreed. Clark's criticisms sounded too much like Thompson's for comfort. In the *Advocate* Ivey warned certain "secular papers" that "every storm of

[87]Raleigh *Progressive Farmer,* July 26, 1898. On Thompson's authorship of the *Progressive Farmer*'s Clark-Kilgo editorials, see Josiah Bailey to Kilgo, July 7, 1898, Trinity College Papers.

[88]The *Biblical Recorder* (Sept. 28, 1898), for one, saw the significance of what Clark was trying to do.

malignant prejudice that howls around our institutions and men only plants them more firmly on the rock of success and makes them nearer and dearer to the great Methodist heart." *Webster's Weekly* finally admitted that "one of the painful features" of the whole controversy was that "many ministers have lost their heads completely and are striking blindly at everybody who opposes Kilgo's reckless policy. They fail to see the principles at stake."[89]

But Clark had another ace up his sleeve which he hoped would influence the two Methodist conferences meeting in November. On September 1 he informed his friend McIver that over half of the endowment that Trinity had received from the Dukes was in the form of American Tobacco Company stock. This could be a sensitive issue indeed, especially since the western conference had passed a resolution against the sale, manufacture and use of cigarettes. Kilgo had all along defended taking the Dukes' money, for, he argued, the church "sanctifies it to a noble end."[90] But ownership of stock in the cigarette trust was, or at least to many people seemed to be, something quite different. As rumors about the stock began to circulate, the first reaction of both Southgate and Ivey, who was also a Trinity trustee, was to deny them.[91] But J. B. Whitaker, the editor of the Winston *Sentinel* and a Clark supporter, was so persistent in his questioning that editor Furman of the *Morning Post,* along with Brown, Odell, and Ivey, finally convinced Southgate that the only way to avoid further damage was to give the facts.[92] Accordingly, on September 23 Southgate informed Whitaker that in November 1897 Washington Duke "set aside for the benefit of Trinity College $100,000 of his property consisting of 910 shares of the preferred stock in the American Tobacco Company." Southgate insisted, however, that the stock was controlled by a special trustee and that the college did not

[89]*Report of the [Clark-Kilgo] Investigation,* p. 46; *North Carolina Christian Advocate,* July 13, 1898; Reidsville *Webster's Weekly,* Oct. 6, 1898.

[90]Clark to McIver, Sept. 1, 1898, McIver Papers; *Minutes of the Western North Carolina Annual Conference . . . 1897,* p. 19; Kilgo in the *North Carolina Christian Advocate,* Oct. 9, 1895.

[91]A. S. Webb to Southgate, Sept. 4, Sept. 7, 1898, and Southgate to Webb, Sept. 9, 1898 (copy), Trinity College Papers; *North Carolina Christian Advocate,* Sept. 14, 1898. See also W. S. Creasy to Kilgo, Sept. 12, 1898, Trinity College Papers.

[92]Whitaker to Southgate, Sept. 16, Sept. 20, 1898, Furman to Southgate, Sept. 21, 1898, Ivey to Southgate, Sept. 22, 1898, Brown to Southgate, Sept. 22, 1898, and Odell to Southgate, Sept. 23, 1898, Trinity College Papers.

own it in a strictly legal sense.[93] Immediately the newspapers broke the whole story. *Webster's Weekly,* for one, was not satisfied with Southgate's subtle distinctions. Trinity's "dividends depend upon the trust's success in selling cigarettes," the *Weekly* declared, "and no amount of sophistry can alter that ugly fact."[94]

The disclosure made things somewhat more difficult for Kilgo and his friends. In the *Advocate* Ivey defended the college with the assurance that the trustees had not conspired to deceive anyone or to withhold the facts. The business wing of the Democracy was primarily concerned about the need to maintain Methodist harmony under Kilgo's leadership. The *Morning Post* proclaimed, "Let the Rich Give," and spoke darkly of the dangers of Methodist division. The Charlotte *Observer,* which had hitherto assumed a position of strict neutrality between Clark and Kilgo, now declared that the unity of the Methodist church, with its "tremendous influence upon the public thought of the State," was essential. Odell, Trinity's principal capitalist supporter in the West, had warned Kilgo earlier about some "very weak-kneed preachers" in the western conference and urged him to attend "as many of the District conferences in the West as you can and especially where things are at all doubtful."[95] In October, L. W. Crawford, the western editor of the *Advocate,* berated Kilgo for keeping the information about the stock secret. He urged Duke to change the form of his gift; for if he did not, the western conference might have to reexamine its connection with Trinity College. Even Bailey was "disturbed about the nature of the Duke gift." Although in a different spirit, he gave Kilgo the same advice that Crawford had given. "To make the change," the Baptist editor confided, "will break the backbone of the trouble."[96]

Kilgo and the trustees had already decided that such a change was the only course, making a tactical concession and thereby

[93]Southgate to Whitaker, Sept. 23, 1898 (copy), ibid.

[94]Raleigh *News and Observer,* Sept. 25, 1898; Raleigh *Morning Post,* Sept. 25, 1898; Reidsville *Webster's Weekly,* Sept. 29, Oct. 13, 1898.

[95]*North Carolina Christian Advocate,* Oct. 19, 1898; Raleigh *Morning Post,* Oct. 6, Oct. 28, 1898; Charlotte *Observer,* Dec. 9, 1898 (see also June 27, Sept. 24, 1898); Odell to Kilgo, July 4, 1898, Trinity College Papers. See also F. A. Bishop to Kilgo, Oct. 14, 1898, ibid.

[96]*North Carolina Christian Advocate,* Oct. 5, 1898; Bailey to Kilgo, Oct. 1898, Trinity College Papers.

gaining a strategic victory.[97] At the western conference late in November, when members raised questions about Trinity's endowment, Kilgo was able to say that Duke had changed the 910 shares into a cash donation. The news was "gladly received"; Bishop Fitzgerald expressed "great satisfaction"; and the conference "joined in singing 'All Hail the Power of Jesus' Name.'"[98] A motion was made that the members again go on record against the sale and manufacture of cigarettes, but as a capstone to Kilgo's victory, it was voted down in favor of a much milder substitute that simply urged preachers to discourage smoking. On the other hand, the conference also refused to endorse a movement led by the Reverend W. C. Wilson and Odell to oust Crawford from his post on the *Advocate*.[99] According to the Charlotte *Observer*, the debate over Crawford prompted "the most heated discussion in the history of the Western North Carolina Conference."[100] Instead, the eastern conference soon resuscitated the old Raleigh *Christian Advocate* and placed it under Ivey's management. In general Odell was pleased with the outcome of the western meeting. "I feel," he wrote Kilgo, ". . . that the tide is changing our way, and the secular press and the Politicians will be 'mum' for awhile at least. I think the backbone of some of our brethren in the West will be stiffened somewhat."[101]

Kingsbury, Webster, Clark, and their supporters were unable to undermine significantly Kilgo's powerful position in the Methodist church. Their failure did not mean, however, that most Methodists fully accepted or even understood the implications of Kilgo's activist policies. Kilgo himself harbored contempt for those he once called "little two by four ecclesiastics," preachers whose vision did not extend beyond the church's traditional spiritual mission.[102] Many of these preachers may have supported Kilgo simply because they accepted his claim that he was the embattled defender of the church and its institutions against a "godless" university

[97]T. N. Ivey to B. N. Duke, Oct. 7, 1898, Duke Papers; Ivey to Kilgo, Oct. 15, 1898, Trinity College Papers.

[98]*North Carolina Christian Advocate*, Nov. 23, 1898.

[99]Reidsville *Webster's Weekly*, Nov. 24, 1898; Charlotte *Observer*, Nov. 23, 1898.

[100]Ibid., Nov. 22, 1898.

[101]*Journal of the North Carolina Annual Conference . . . 1898*, pp. 26, 51; ibid. (1899), pp. 51-53; Odell to Kilgo, Dec. 7, 1898, Trinity College Papers.

[102]W. H. L. McLaurin (who quotes Kilgo) to Kilgo, Oct. 11, 1897, ibid.

or "wreckers" like Clark. This kind of reaction was, of course, less likely to occur in the western conference, which was still smarting from Trinity's move to Durham. The charge that Kilgo was prostituting the church to business interests elicited a sympathetic response from those Methodists who were convinced that corporate greed was responsible for the state's poverty or who believed that the capitalist values of the New South were subverting traditional morality and the virtues of the Old South. But other Methodists were grateful for the benevolence of businessmen like the Dukes who endowed colleges and helped build churches. For them the factory builders were but the instruments of an inscrutable and wise Providence.

Kilgo's strength lay partly in the very ambiguity of his commitments. He was a great Wesleyan preacher, vehement in denouncing the liquor traffic or the immorality bred by state higher education. At the same time he was propounding what was in effect a social gospel for the New South, calling upon the church to play an active part in assuring the triumph of a progressive capitalist civilization. In the peculiar circumstances of the postbellum South—in many ways still an underdeveloped region—it was the men at Trinity, in the company of prophets like Walter Hines Page and William Garrott Brown, who considered themselves the liberals, the progressives, in the vanguard of change. In 1897 Bassett had anticipated a time when "the intelligent people" of North Carolina would finally accept Trinity's "mission" as a broadening and liberalizing influence.[103] Tarheel businessmen and their political allies clearly accepted it in 1898. They knew what Kilgo was about.

[103]Quoted in Nannie M. Tilley, *The Trinity College Historical Society, 1892-1941* (Durham, 1941), p. 58. See also Edwin Mims to W. H. Page, Nov. 24, 1903, Page Papers.

VII

White Supremacy

ONE THING that conservatives and businessmen wanted in 1898 was a restoration of political stability after years of agrarian agitation and fusion rule. The Democratic leadership,* dominated by probusiness elements, rejected cooperation with the Populists and determined upon a "straight-out" fight that year to regain power. Despite concessions the party platform made to Populist concerns, the Democrats directed the thrust of their campaign to denouncing the outrages of "Negro rule." White supremacy became the rallying cry around which all factions in the party could unite. Neopopulist Democrats, who were then supporting Clark in his controversy with Kilgo, had no choice but to go along, and white supremacy was so potent an issue that they generally did so with enthusiasm. The white supremacy campaign and the Clark-Kilgo affair offered a strange counterpoint: the one based upon a unifying consensus, the other, on class politics. The Morganton *Farmer's Friend*, a supporter of Clark, distinguished between the two, sounded a note of warning, but perceived no real contradiction: "We are now in the midst of a fight for the supremacy of the white race in North Carolina with every prospect of winning it. It will be a chill wind down the spinal marrow to have it suspected that the beneficiaries of the victory will be the corporations and trusts, whose enmity Judge Clark has incurred and who now strike at him through his church."[1]

Other Democrats were glad to see class issues take second place. The *Manufacturers' Record,* approvingly quoted by the Charlotte

---

[1]Sept. 8, 1898. For discussions of the white supremacy campaign, see Josephus Daniels, *Editor in Politics* (Chapel Hill, 1941), pp. 283-312; Helen G. Edmonds, *The Negro and Fusion Politics in North Carolina, 1894-1901* (Chapel Hill, 1951), pp. 136-57; Oliver H. Orr, Jr., *Charles Brantley Aycock* (Chapel Hill, 1961), pp. 111-42; Joseph L. Morrison, *Josephus Daniels Says . . . : An Editor's Political Odyssey from Bryan to Wilson and F.D.R., 1894-1913* (Chapel Hill, 1962), pp. 104-14; and Joseph Flake Steelman, "The Progressive Era in North Carolina, 1884-1917" (Ph.D. diss., University of North Carolina, 1955), pp. 156-96.

Observer, reminded its Tarheel readers that with "possible negro control, all other questions, be they finance, tariff or expansion, sink into insignificance." Everyone—businessmen, laborers, farmers—had a vital interest in uniting behind the white supremacy party, reasoned the *Morning Post*.[2] Many Tarheels were convinced that white supremacy would make the New South vision of progress and economic development a reality. To Charles Brantley Aycock white supremacy as progressive reform meant "a larger political freedom and a greater toleration of opinion. . . . The Democratic party will be set free from the trammels of the race issue and can enter upon a career of economic study and legislation."[3] One theme articulated by all Democrats was that their campaign represented something more than mere partisanship. They identified themselves with a traditional southern ethos, calling into play the old shibboleths of race, the Anglo-Saxon mystique, and, not least, the South's religiosity. According to one Democratic legislator, the two "cardinal principles of Democracy" were "the Christian religion" and "white supremacy."[4] The Democrats, the defenders of civilization, were the only party of "intelligence, virtue and property."[5] Daniels saw the campaign as "a righteous struggle," "something far above politics," "a sort of protection of home."[6] "The redemption of North Carolina," the Wilmington *Messenger* intoned, "is the imperative demand of civilization and honor and liberty itself."[7]

In this great work the churches were to take a prominent part. Ideological conflict had torn into the denominations as much as into the whole body politic. The doctrine of the spiritual nature of the church was in shambles. But in 1898 that did not seem to matter. White supremacy, civilization itself, was everybody's business. Daniels earlier had defended the purity of religion against Populist attacks; he had criticized ministers who openly advocated Populist doctrine, as well as denominational spokesmen against

[2]Charlotte *Observer,* Nov. 14, 1898; Raleigh *Morning Post,* Nov. 2, Nov. 8, 1898.

[3]Quoted in Orr, p. 150.

[4]Quoted in Raleigh *News and Observer,* Mar. 7, 1899.

[5]B. H. Tyson to Henry G. Connor, [1898], Connor Papers, Southern Hist. Coll., UNC Lib.

[6]P. 283.

[7]Aug. 25, 1897. Aycock carried the same message in his campaign speeches across the state (Orr, pp. 126-27).

state aid, for forsaking their spiritual tasks in favor of politics. But, as if all the controversies of the decade had passed from memory, he presented the election of 1898 as one of those critical moments, like the slavery controversy or Reconstruction, when the churches had to take a stand, when the public assertion of clerical authority was no longer a matter of politics but of morality and duty of the highest order. "When prominent ministers speak out on political questions," the *News and Observer* declared, ". . . it will be found that something more is at stake than mere party triumph. . . . [They] support the contention . . . that the Democratic party is making a fight for civilization and morality, not for office." As Daniels saw it, the cause of religion itself was at stake. The church and the Democratic party, the *News and Observer* insisted, "will save us—for time and eternity, if we will heed their admonitions."[8]

Such were the assumptions that doubtless impelled many preachers to join the white supremacy movement. In vain did the Republican Asheville *Register* denounce "flannel-mouthed so-called ministers of the Gospel, who so forget their calling as to go up and down the country roaring their foul slanders and vicious falsehoods for political effect in a worse and more vindictive manner than is possible for a common cross-roads politician to do."[9] Preachers, along with other citizens of "high standing," patrolled black neighborhoods in Raleigh in the days before the election.[10] Newspapers gave wide publicity to preachers who helped expose the supposed infamies of black rule. The Reverend O. L. Stringfield, financial agent of the Baptist Female University, spoke to the Kings Mountain Baptist Association of God's purposes for the Anglo-Saxon race and asserted that "not one twentieth of the horrors of negro domination had been published in the papers." The Cleveland *Star* endorsed Stringfield's remarks, adding that no one would dare say that "ministers of the gospel would be guilty of assisting in circulating what some worthies are pleased to term 'Democratic lies.'" When the Reverend Jesse Page,

[8]Oct. 6, 1898, Dec. 1, 1897. See also July 23, Nov. 28, 1897; Fayetteville *Observer,* Oct. 19, 1898; and an appeal by Professor Jerome Dowd of Trinity in the Concord *Standard,* Nov. 2, 1898.

[9]Quoted in Raleigh *Morning Post,* Oct. 22, 1898. See also Winston *Union Republican,* Aug. 11, 1898; Raleigh *Progressive Farmer,* July 19, 1898.

[10]Daniels, p. 288.

an uncle of Walter Hines Page, and the Reverend R. F. Campbell, a Wilmington Presbyterian minister, urged that white men vote against all Populist and Republican candidates, the Charlotte *Observer* remarked, "Therefore it is the clearest evidence that the State of North Carolina is in danger from political self-seekers, when the most earnest, careful, conservative ministers of the Gospel use their pulpits to urge upon their people the duties of citizenship at the present time."[11]

The Reverend C. W. Blanchard, a Baptist of Kinston, admitted that it was "doubtless best for a minister of the Gospel to be as non-partisan in his politics as possible," but he felt compelled to speak out when he noticed that "our white daughters can't walk the streets, free from the insults that a stripling negro girl, as black as the ace of spades, much younger than themselves, is to heap upon them."[12] The Reverend T. H. Leavitt of Fayetteville resurrected the old biblical arguments for slavery and tried to prove that black people had to subordinate themselves to the white race. He stood "with the Anglo-Saxon party without fusion or garble."[13] At a huge white supremacy rally in Goldsboro just before the election, the Reverend N. M. Jurney, a prominent Methodist and trustee of Trinity College, invoked divine blessing on the movement and erased any distinction between what promised to be a sweeping Democratic victory at the polls and a moral and spiritual rebirth: "Look down upon this vast assemblage of people who are gathered here in the interest of peace and good government towards all men. . . . Let us feel this day the vibrations of our coming redemption from all wicked rule, and the supremacy of that race destined not only to rule this country but to carry the Gospel to all nations and maintain Civil and Religious Liberty throughout the world." The rally adopted a resolution offered by Jurney demanding that all businesses suspend operations on election day and "give the entire day to the service of white supremacy."[14]

[11]Cleveland *Star* quoted in Raleigh *News and Observer*, Oct. 4, 1898; Charlotte *Observer*, Oct. 8, 1898. See also ibid., Oct. 16, Oct. 23, 1898; Raleigh *News and Observer*, Sept. 9, Oct. 6, Oct. 20, 1898; Statesville *Mascot*, Sept. 8, 1898; Wilmington *Star*, Sept. 7, 1898.

[12]Kinston *Free Press* quoted in Concord *Standard*, Sept. 24, 1898.

[13]Fayetteville *Observer*, Oct. 19, 1898.

[14]Raleigh *Morning Post*, Oct. 30, 1898. See also Daniels, p. 300.

Two days after the election a white-instigated race riot broke out at Wilmington in which between eleven and thirty black people perished. Threatened by the Democrats with further violence, all Republican city officials resigned and handed over power to their opponents. The new Democratic mayor, Alfred Moore Waddell, had earlier boasted about "choking" the Cape Fear River with black corpses.[15] The Reverend Mr. Crawford of the *Advocate* considered the incident "unfortunate" but praised the "ability and zeal" of the Democrats. For once agreeing with his western colleague on the *Advocate,* editor Ivey admired "the forebearance of the white citizens of Wilmington during ante-election days." He too wished the transition of power could have been peaceful. "But," he concluded, "we will not criticize. We will thank God that it was no worse, and thank Him that the vexing problem has been solved."[16] Peyton Hoge, pastor of the city's First Presbyterian Church, told his congregation that Waddell and his fellow Democrats had "redeemed Wilmington civilization, law, order, decency, and responsibility." Other Wilmington ministers concurred in this judgment.[17] Responding in the *Independent,* an important New York Protestant journal, to widespread northern press criticism of Democratic tactics, the Reverend Alexander J. McKelway, editor of the Charlotte *Presbyterian Standard,* defended the Democrats and excused the violence in Wilmington. "Lawlessness reigned," he argued, "because the intelligence, the courage, the property and character of the city had been defied." Editorially taking issue with the North Carolina minister, the *Independent* noted, "Even in the pulpit one will hear God thanked for the accomplishment of deeds that ought to make a man blush."[18] The Charlotte *Observer* then defended McKelway and accused the *Independent* of exhibiting "sectionalism, partisanship, and meanness."[19]

[15] The best treatment of the riot is Edmonds, pp. 158-77.

[16] *North Carolina Christian Advocate,* Nov. 16, 1898.

[17] Raleigh *Morning Post,* Nov. 15, 1898; Charlotte *Observer,* Nov. 17, 1898.

[18] McKelway, "The Causes of the Troubles in North Carolina," *Independent* 50 (Nov. 24, 1898): 1488-92. For the *Independent*'s response, see ibid., p. 1514. See also McKelway, "The North Carolina Revolution Justified," *Outlook* 60 (Dec. 31, 1898): 1057-59.

[19] Nov. 30, 1898.

White supremacy represented consensual politics reduced to its least common denominator. The contrived nature of the unity within both Democratic and denominational ranks was no more apparent than in the way the state aid issue was manipulated out of the political arena. Bailey, White, Kilgo, and their followers had asserted a new political independence for the churches in the fight over appropriations to higher education and in the process had estranged themselves from many Democrats who were strongly committed to the university and the other state colleges. The possibility existed of a considerable defection of the proponents of Christian education from what one Methodist minister contemptuously called "State Aid Democracy."[20]

As early as March 1897 Thomas M. Pittman, a lawyer and prominent Baptist—and no particular friend of Bailey's—warned A. W. Graham of the possible consequences for the Democrats if something were not done about the denominations' contention that the state should not appropriate money to the university:

Now without discussing here the correctness of that contention, the fact of its existence is most undesirable. I have no doubt that it has contributed to the present deplorable political situation. It is useless to speak of the criticism stopping without some adjustment of the controversy. It would simply be "eating crow" and Bailey is neither by inheritance nor training disposed to that. . . . I add . . . that I do not believe the Democratic party will early regain power in North Carolina until the University question is settled.[21]

Bailey's *Biblical Recorder* was, after all, the official organ of North Carolina Baptists and enjoyed a rather large circulation which grew from 5,000 in 1893 to 9,000 in 1903.[22] It would have been unfortunate indeed if the *Recorder*, which, unlike other denominational papers, was never reluctant to address itself to political issues, assumed a hostile or lukewarm attitude toward Democratic ambitions. The issue of university appropriations represented an exposed flank for the Democratic party.

[20]L. J. Holden to J. C. Kilgo, Aug. 28, 1898, Trinity College Papers, Duke Univ. Archives.

[21]Pittman to Graham, Mar. 5, 1897, Graham Papers, Southern Hist. Coll., UNC Lib. On Pittman's relations with Bailey, see Pittman to Bailey, Mar. 18, 1902, Pittman Papers, Southern Hist. Coll., UNC Lib.

[22]*Biblical Recorder*, Sept. 9, 1903, May 1, 1907. Bailey claimed that the *Recorder* had a larger circulation than any other paper in the state (Bailey to W. H. Page, Dec. 23, 1903, Page Papers, Houghton Lib., Harvard Univ.).

Party Chairman Simmons sensed the danger—or at least he was taking no chances—when he decided to accommodate denominational grievances for the sake of Democratic unity. In his memoirs Simmons later recalled: "I promised the various denominational colleges which were then rather hostile to the State institutions, that I would not increase the appropriations for the latter during the session of 1899. . . . If we we were to win, every controversy which tended to divide the Democratic vote had to be held in abeyance."[23] The men involved in the state aid deal, besides Simmons, were Bailey, White, and possibly former Governor Jarvis.[24]

Up to this point Bailey had always claimed to be nonpartisan, probably in order to obtain support for the "voluntary principle" wherever he could find it. The editor had always urged Baptists to put their principles above party. Still, until 1898 Bailey kept at least one foot in the fusion camp. After all, a sizable minority of Populists, despite the attitude of their leaders, had opposed state aid in the legislature of 1897. The *Biblical Recorder* gave high praise to the inaugural address of Republican Governor Daniel L. Russell in 1897. Although Russell urged a continuation of state aid, Bailey took comfort from the fact that the governor did not openly condemn the university's opponents as, by implication, the Democrats did. Furthermore, the *Biblical Recorder* sharply criticized those who accused Russell of "toadyism" to vested interests.[25] Not long afterwards the governor rewarded Bailey with a seat on the North Carolina Board of Agriculture.[26] Bailey's nonpartisanship had placed him inside the fusion administration itself.

It is likely that Simmons first approached Bailey about a compromise on state aid shortly after the state Democratic convention in May 1898, for up to that time the Baptist editor was as busy as ever preparing the hosts to do battle against the university in the upcoming campaign.[27] Presumably in return for Simmons's favors

[23]*F. M. Simmons, Statesman of the New South: Memoirs and Addresses*, ed. J. Fred Rippy (Durham, 1936), p. 29.

[24]According to Daniels, the "secret conference" included Bailey, White, Simmons, Jarvis, "and others" (p. 319). In the extant correspondence between Bailey and Kilgo in 1898 there is no mention of the deal.

[25]*Biblical Recorder*, Jan. 1, Oct. 7, Nov. 4, 1896, Jan. 20, 1897.

[26]Raleigh *News and Observer*, June 18, 1897.

[27]Bailey to Kilgo, Mar. 28, 1898, Trinity College Papers; *Biblical Recorder*, Mar. 30, 1898.

Bailey and his comrades were expected to let up on the attack. By the end of May the *Recorder* had assumed a more conciliatory tone toward the whole state aid issue.[28] There were probably other aspects to the bargain as well, for Bailey quickly began to play an active role in the Democratic campaign.

Probably as a part of his deal with Simmons, Bailey dramatically resigned from the board of agriculture in the summer of 1898. This followed close on the heels of charges by Simmons of corruption in the Russell administration involving the board and the state penitentiary. Earlier Bailey had introduced resolutions demanding that the commissioner of agriculture, who had previously served as superintendent of the penitentiary, resign. It is likely that Simmons got his inside information to expose the alleged corruption from Bailey.[29] Simmons regarded the exposure of the scandal and especially Bailey's resignation as a great boon to the Democrats. Daniels later speculated that Bailey resigned from the board because he had "lost influence" by cooperating with fusion, but the Raleigh editor also admitted that his action was "widely used" by the Democrats in the campaign.[30] In fact, the *News and Observer,* which had never had much use for Bailey, praised his actions effusively, not failing to point out the he had never taken part in "partisan politics."[31] Bailey's nonpartisanship, of course, made his revelations that much more effective. The *Morning Post* for once agreed entirely with its Raleigh rival.[32] A more skeptical reader, however, called Bailey's effort "a grand strike in order to court the favor of the Democratic party."[33] The fusionist press was amused at Bailey's sudden conversion to the Democratic cause. The *Progressive Farmer* warned the Baptist editor that "he can't serve God and Chairman Simmons of the Democratic campaign committee at the same time."[34] But in

[28]May 25, 1898. See also Daniels, p. 318.

[29]On Simmons's exposure and Bailey's resignation, see ibid., Dec. 15, 1897, June 17, July 28, July 31, 1898; Raleigh *Morning Post,* July 31, 1898; *Biblical Recorder,* Aug. 10, 1898.

[30]*F. M. Simmons,* p. 22; Daniels, pp. 318-19.   [31]July 31, 1898.

[32]July 31, 1898. See also New Bern *Daily Journal,* Aug. 2, 1898.

[33]M. I. Stewart to the Raleigh *Morning Post,* Aug. 1, 1898.

[34]Aug. 6, 1898. See also July 19, July 26, Aug. 2, Aug. 9, Aug. 23, Sept. 13, 1898; Raleigh *Caucasian,* July 28, 1898; Winston *Union Republican,* Aug. 11, 1898; *Biblical Recorder,* July 13, Oct. 26, 1898.

opting for Simmons, Bailey was choosing a power-
ful terrestrial ally. His isolation from men of influence, which
seemed to be the case after August 1897, was coming to an end.

Bailey entered the white supremacy campaign with a record of
ambiguous pronouncements on the race issue. He condemned
lynching while insisting that the only remedy for the evil was a
more vigorous enforcement of the law against rapists. He opposed
disfranchisement in South Carolina in 1895 but doubted the
capacity of blacks to use the ballot intelligently. Early in 1897 he
observed that the black men in the North Carolina legislature were
more intelligent than many of the whites they represented, but
later in the same year he denounced black politicians as "a motley,
thirsty, hungry, demagog-fired crew." As late as February 1898
the *Biblical Recorder* proclaimed the black man "a voter and forever," but in the weeks before the election it was proudly riding
the white supremacy bandwagon. Bailey charged that the "dread
of negro rule has kept the people of North Carolina from that freedom of voting which is the soul of political progress." After the
election he found the hearts of the men who led the Wilmington
"revolution" pure and their cause just.[35]

During the campaign Populists and Republicans repeatedly
charged that if the Democrats regained power, they would devise a
scheme to restrict the suffrage similar to those already adopted by
several southern states. This would be done in the name of white
supremacy, but it would have the effect of taking away the vote
from poor, illiterate white men. Most Democrats, including the
state committee, emphatically denied the charge and ridiculed the
"bogeyman" and "scarecrow" of disfranchisement.[36] Bailey, however, was still asserting some of his political independence. He
departed from the official Democratic line by advocating an "illiteracy law" as the "only solution" to the suffrage problem. A law
denying illiterates the right to vote would purify the electorate
and be the best possible stimulus to improving public education.[37]
According to the Winston *Union Republican,* Bailey's statements
proved that the "machine Democrats" intended to exclude all

[35]Mar. 31, 1897, Aug. 21, Oct. 2, 1895, Feb. 24, Nov. 17, 1897, Feb. 16, Oct. 26,
1898 (see also Aug. 10, Sept. 7, 1898), Nov. 16, 1898.

[36]Reidsville *Webster's Weekly,* Sept. 29, 1898; Charlotte *Observer,* Oct. 25, 1898;
Edmonds, *The Negro and Fusion Politics,* pp. 140-41.

[37]*Biblical Recorder,* Oct. 26, July 6, Sept. 28, 1898.

"good men" who might happen to be illiterate. "Bro. Bailey," it concluded, "is evidently full in keeping with the spirit of the 'Democratic times.'"[38]

John C. Kilgo was even more blunt than his Baptist friend. He told his students that circumstances required all good citizens to support white supremacy. He insisted, however, that "the supreme question should be good government" and that he himself went "as a quarry slave under no political lash." "No man has a right to rule who has not a fitness to rule," Kilgo declared, adding, "That excludes a good many white people." "We want good government where the best class rules and where the intelligence and culture and strength of this state is in authority."[39] For both Bailey and Kilgo, then, white supremacy transcended the issue of race. If their remarks during the campaign are taken in context with everything else they had been saying up to then, white supremacy meant for them an orderly but progressive administration of public affairs by an elite committed to the development of the state.

White supremacy, by obscuring the factional discord between conservative, New South, and neopopulist Democrats, propelled the party to an impressive victory in November. It elected 134 representatives and senators against 30 for the Republicans and only 6 for the Populists. The fusionists' worst fears were realized when the legislature took up disfranchisement as the first order of business. A legislative committee spent a month hammering out a constitutional amendment which passed both houses by wide margins. It provided for literacy qualifications for voting, but to protect white illiterates it also contained a grandfather clause exempting all those registering before December 1908 who either had voted or were descendants of anyone who had voted in any state election before 1867. In addition, the legislature revised the election law to insure Democratic control of the polls. The voters would have the opportunity to approve or reject the amendment in August 1900.[40]

[38]Oct. 6, 1898.

[39]"Dr. Kilgo's Chapel Talk to the Students," Oct. 28, 1898, typescript in the Kilgo Papers, Duke Univ. Archives. See also an untitled typescript, Nov. 9, 1898, ibid.

[40]On the legislative session of 1899 and the drafting of the amendment, see Daniels, pp. 324-27; Edmonds, pp. 178-97; William Alexander Mabry, "'White Supremacy' and the North Carolina Suffrage Amendment," *North Carolina Historical Review* 13 (1936): 1-24. The legislature changed the date of voting for all state offices to August so that national affairs might not obtrude on the overriding issue at hand.

The grandfather clause, which must have disappointed people like Bailey and Kilgo, was a politically necessary device to assure mass white electoral support for the amendment. Bailey had anticipated correctly that a literacy qualification for voting would also arouse renewed interest in the public schools. The Democrats, who had decisively undercut the local taxation campaign of 1897, became sudden converts to the cause of universal education. "It was stated by several members," the Charlotte *Observer* reported, "that they wanted every white boy to read and write by 1908." When Charles Dabney later asserted that the Democrats had been "chastened and impressed by the demands of the plain people." he was only partly correct. The chastening process was intensified by their fear for the amendment's fate in the face of charges that it would disfranchise white illiterates. The Democrats had good political reasons to enter the campaign of 1900 as the party of educational reform.[41]

Also ignoring the disfranchisement issue, the Baptist historian George W. Paschal asserted that his denomination had so effectively aroused the state to a perception of its educational needs that the Democrats had no choice but to go along.[42] There is no question that both Baptists and Methodists, along with such educational reformers as Alderman, McIver, and Mebane, were instrumental in making the deplorable condition of the schools a matter of public concern. Denominational efforts derived partly from tactical considerations in their concurrent battle against state aid to higher education. The state, they insisted, could not afford to support both public schools and a university. But defenders of the university were wrong in charging that denominational solicitude for the schools amounted to little more than hypocrisy. The idealism of the churchmen and their concern for the schools certainly appear to have been genuine. Although they may have had little sympathy for Populist measures, their faith in the regenerative powers of education for the poor was nonetheless strong. "Those who travel to any great extent in the State," observed Charles E. Taylor

[41]Charlotte *Observer*, Mar. 7, 1899; Charles W. Dabney, *Universal Education in the South*, 2 vols. (Chapel Hill, 1939), 1: 214; Louis R. Harlan, *Separate and Unequal: Public School Campaigns and Racism in the Southern Seaboard States, 1901-1905* (paperback ed.; New York, 1968), pp. 60-74.

[42]Paschal, "The Truth as to the Public School Advancement in North Carolina," *The Wake Forest Student* 47 (1929): 58.

in his anti-state-aid pamphlet of 1894, "and are brought into con-
tact with the people in the rural districts know far better what the
real illiteracy is than can be discovered from any table of statistics.
There are multitudes, white as well as black, who can neither read
nor write. And many of these people have little desire that their
children should learn."[43] If anything, the political involvement of
churchmen in the state aid fight seems to have encouraged them to
go a step further toward breaking down their traditional inhibi-
tions against speaking out on controversial public questions.
Everyone, of course, agreed that public education needed improvement—to that extent it was hardly a controversial issue. But the
local taxation campaign of 1897 showed that it could become so
in a particular political context. Bailey and other denominational
leaders played a very active role in the 1897 campaign and very
nearly came to grief on that account.

Paschal also endorsed Bailey's contention, first made in the fall
of 1897, that the fusionists were responsible for the failure of
local taxation.[44] Bailey knew perfectly well, as he later indicated,
that the Democrats had defeated it.[45] As he perceived the drift of
events during and after the local taxation campaign, Bailey quite
possibly realized that he ought to begin reestablishing his ties to
the Democratic party, a realization that culminated in his deal
with Simmons. Or as Paschal put it, "Mr. Bailey, whose powerful
influence was now recognized and courted by the able politicians
of the day, had grown in wisdom—he had allied himself and his
cause with Simmons and Aycock."[46] Bailey's "wisdom" in fact
amounted to a recognition of certain limits. He had tried to ignore
the race issue in 1897. But it was precisely the cry of "white supremacy" that the Democrats raised so effectively to defeat local

[43]Taylor, *How Far Should a State Undertake to Educate? or, A Plea for the Voluntary System in Higher Education* (Raleigh, 1894), p. 21. See also *Minutes of the Annual
Meeting of the Baptist State Convention of North Carolina . . . 1895*, p. 70; *Biblical
Recorder,* May 2, 1894; Columbus Durham to the Raleigh *News and Observer,* Sept. 28,
1894.

[44]Paschal, p. 58. See also *Biblical Recorder* quoted in the Raleigh *News and Observer,* Sept. 1, 1897.

[45]Joseph [Josiah] W. Bailey, "Popular Education and the Race Problem in North
Carolina," *The Outlook* 68 (May 11, 1901): 114-15. Bailey also pointed out here that
political circumstances forced the Democrats to take a stand on behalf of public education.

[46]Paschal, p. 58.

taxation and that in 1898 helped propel them back into power. What Bailey and other denominational supporters of public schools did, once they realized their isolation from their own constituencies in 1897, was to help the Democrats combine white supremacy and educational idealism into a winning package. The educational idealism had been compromised by the latent racism of Tarheel Protestants.

State aid to higher education was also a factor in Bailey's calculations, and that issue proved inseparable from the public school question in the legislative session of 1899. Democrat Locke Craig, apparently unaware of Simmons's agreement with Bailey, assured Alderman that the "University can get anything it wants from this legislature."[47] He was sadly mistaken. In any case the Democrats were determined to keep expenditures low.[48] The desire for economy reinforced the denominational argument that money "wasted" on higher education could be put to better use in the public schools. While Bailey agitated the education issue in the *Recorder,* White was busy pledging candidates. "Will you put the common schools first in appropriations for education?" he asked. "Will you favor legislation to carry out as fast and as far as possible the mandatory c[l]ause of the constitution [requiring a four-month term]?" In White's office at the Mission Board of the Baptist convention, Superintendent Mebane drew up a bill to appropriate $100,000 for improvement of the state's school system.[49] The *Biblical Recorder* immediately endorsed Mebane's proposals.[50] Alderman and McIver argued before the joint committee on education that $100,000 would not significantly help the schools but might deny funds needed for the training of teachers in the state's institutions of higher learning. They urged instead a continuation of the local taxation provision of the 1897

[47]Craig to Alderman, Nov. 23, 1898, University of North Carolina Papers, UNC Archives.

[48]Joseph P. Caldwell to Alderman, Jan. 9, 1899, ibid. This was also an aspect of Simmons's deal with the corporations.

[49]John Ellington White, "When the Tide Began to Turn for Popular Education in North Carolina, 1890-1900," State Literary and Historical Association of North Carolina, *Proceedings* (1922), no. 1 (1923), pp. 40-41.

[50]Nov. 9, 1898.

law.[51] When the committee on appropriations was hearing arguments for an increase in state aid, White bluntly told the members
of Simmons's pledges in order "to get the State aid issue out of
politics."[52] McIver was mortified when he learned of the bargain.
But John B. Holman, the Baptist sponsor of the $100,000 bill in
the house, was "delighted." "By heavens, Simmons," he said,
"hold them to the promises!"[53]

Simmons did. The legislature made no increase in the regular
appropriations to the university and the state colleges, providing
only an additional $12,500 for the installation of waterworks at
Chapel Hill and for other capital improvements.[54] According to
White, he and Bailey were "as generous as possible under the
circumstances."[55] The $100,000 school bill also passed both
houses almost unanimously. But the money was to be distributed
to the counties not on the basis of need but according to school
age population. The Democrats also repealed the local taxation
law of 1897.[56] Despite these shortcomings, the *News and Observer*
hailed the measure as the "most important bill for popular education that has been enacted in a decade."[57] The *Biblical Recorder*
regarded it "as the greatest and noblest change in the State's educational policy."[58]

The only men with cause for regret were Alderman and McIver.
The latter was particularly upset that his friend Daniels had neglected to push for state aid in the *News and Observer* both during the
campaign and while the legislature was in session. He wondered
why Daniels printed the "rot" White told the legislature.[59] Although Daniels has claimed that he knew nothing about the

[51]Raleigh *News and Observer*, Jan. 24, 1899; Daniels, pp. 323-24; and Paschal, pp.
58-59.

[52]As reported in the *Presbyterian Standard* and quoted in Reidsville *Webster's
Weekly*, May 11, 1899.

[53]*F. M. Simmons*, p. 29.   [54]Raleigh *News and Observer*, Mar. 7, Mar. 12, 1899.

[55]P. 41.

[56]Raleigh *News and Observer*, Mar. 7, 1899; Charlotte *Observer*, Mar. 7, 1899;
Samuel A. Thompson, "The Legislative Development of Public School Support in North
Carolina" (Ph.D. diss., University of North Carolina, 1936), pp. 347-48; and Harlan, pp.
62-63.

[57]Mar. 9, 1899.   [58]Mar. 15, 1899.

[59]McIver to Daniels, Mar. 11, 1899, copy in the McIver Papers, Lib. of UNC at
Greensboro.

Bailey-Simmons deal, he perhaps realized instinctively that the Democrats could not afford to agitate the state aid question.[60] Alderman, who had understandably become "very sick of the legislature," left North Carolina a year later to assume the presidency of Tulane University.[61] The amazing thing was that none of the major Democratic newspapers, with the exception of *Webster's Weekly,* editorially criticized the Bailey-Simmons deal once it became known.[62]

The Democrats could now exploit the educational record that Bailey and White had helped them make in 1899. "The best pledge that no white people will be disfranchised by the amendment," Bailey wrote two weeks before the Democratic convention of 1900, "will be a five months school term throughout the Commonwealth." White personally "stood by" and watched as a strong public school plank was typed into the Democratic platform.[63] The stage was set for Charles Brantley Aycock to declare to the convention that nominated him for governor: "With the adoption of our amendment after 1908 there will be no State in the Union with a larger percentage of boys and girls who can read and write, and no State will rush forward with more celerity or certainty than conservative Old North Carolina."[64]

Religious opinion supported the amendment enthusiastically. Preachers helped the Democrats place the campaign on an even loftier plane than that of 1898. The persistence of violence, intimidation, and fraud in the black counties could be conveniently overlooked.[65] The *Biblical Recorder* declared: "We look for a moral revolution in North Carolina. We look for a revision of our

[60]Daniels has claimed that he changed his course in regard to state aid and tried to thwart the denominational leaders' plans when McIver told him about the Bailey-Simmons deal early in the session (pp. 319-20). There was in fact no change in the editorial policy of the *News and Observer* while the legislature was in session, and McIver's letter of Mar. 11, 1899, was sent to Daniels after the lawmakers had adjourned (copy in McIver Papers; see also G. T. Winston to McIver, Mar. 27, 1899, ibid.).

[61]H. A. Foushee to Henry Groves Connor, May 16, 1899, Connor Papers; Dumas Malone, *Edwin A. Alderman: A Biography* (New York, 1940), pp. 95-97.

[62]Reidsville *Webster's Weekly,* May 11, 1899.

[63]*Biblical Recorder,* Mar. 28, 1900; White, p. 43.   [64]Quoted in Orr, p. 159.

[65]For a vivid description of the campaign, see the New York *Times,* July 31, 1900. On the "idealistic" universal education theme, see Edmonds, pp. 204-5 (which stresses the belated Democratic commitment to education); Harlan, pp. 64-68; and Mabry, p. 19.

whole political system." Campaign orators like Aycock even turned a paternalistic gaze toward the black man and urged their fellow whites to exercise justice and moderation.[66] Bailey praised Aycock's message for "its excellence, its force, its candor, its fine spirit, . . . its power," and its sympathy for the soon-to-be disfranchised blacks.[67] Bailey insisted that the amendment "will help the negro who needs help" and that "Christian men and women everywhere will come back to teaching, and helping, and protecting [him]."[68] The *Presbyterian Standard* pictured disfranchisement as liberation for black people, who had been "held in bondage" by "political interests." Once he was out of politics, the black man could "throw himself upon the protection of his masters" and appeal successfully "to all that is noblest in a noble people."[69]

The widely respected Elder P. D. Gold of the Primitive Baptists supported the amendment on the grounds that it would "lift politics out of the filth and mud of party spleen and bitterness."[70] Indeed, according to *Webster's Weekly,* the Primitive Baptists did two things with "religious regularity": they paid their debts and voted Democratic. Elder L. H. Hardy found that the amendment embodied "the very essence of our own church government." "Old Baptists believe in white supremacy in church matters and so do all the churches," Webster added.[71] The *News and Observer* proceeded to read one "renegade" preacher, Baylus Cade, out of the Baptist church for denouncing the amendment and claiming that his coreligionists, Bailey and White, in reality opposed the public schools. The Raleigh daily compared "Decayed Baylus" to Cyrus Thompson who "made himself conspicuous chiefly for his tirade against the Christian churches." It seemed to the *News and Observer* that anyone who joined hands with the blacks was "ready also to slander the church and tear down its good name."[72]

To no one's surprise the amendment and the entire Democratic ticket triumphed at the polls in August 1900. The *North Carolina Christian Advocate* greeted the elimination of "an ignorant and purchasable vote" and anticipated a revival of "the educational

[66]*Biblical Recorder,* July 25, 1900; Orr, p. 178.   [67]*Biblical Recorder,* May 2, 1900.

[68]Quoted in the Raleigh *News and Observer,* July 29, 1900.   [69]June 20, 1900.

[70]Raleigh *News and Observer,* June 10, 1900.   [71]July 19, July 26, 1900.

[72]June 19, 1900. See also June 20, June 23, 1900.

spirit."[73] Businessmen and those conservatives who preferred social stability to the turmoil of the 1890s took seriously the campaign rhetoric which promised that the elimination of the black vote would usher in an era of sound and honest government.[74] Henry Groves Connor of Wilson was perhaps typical of Tarheel conservatives. He had been a judge and, as speaker of the state house of representatives in 1899, an architect of the white supremacy amendment. In that year he told a Trinity College audience that disfranchisement would result in "a saner citizenship" and give "the highest, best and purest motives of both races . . . play and operation." The amendment, he said, " was wrought by men with tears in their eyes."[75] Indeed, the end of the legislative session left Connor "depressed in spirits."[76] He believed that a $300 property qualification should have been included in the amendment to eliminate from the electorate the supposedly vicious elements of both races.[77]

Businessmen contributed much to the campaign and expected to benefit from the consequences. In 1898 one "prominent gentleman," according to the Charlotte *Observer,* went so far as to declare that "business men of the State are largely responsible for the victory." "Not before in years," he stated, "have the bank men, the mill men and the businessmen in general—the backbone of the property interests of the State—taken such sincere interest in affairs." That same year the Republican state chairman, A. E. Holton, complained that "every interest in the state representing capital was arrayed against us."[78] Even Ben Duke, a Republican, had no quarrel with disfranchisement as such; he wished only that "the ignorant white man" had been included.[79] John W. Fries, a leading Winston capitalist, insisted shortly after the passage of the disfranchisement amendment that henceforth businessmen must keep a closer check on political affairs. "The South," he argued,

[73]*North Carolina Christian Advocate,* Aug. 8, 1900. See also Raleigh *Christian Advocate* quoted in Raleigh *News and Observer,* Aug. 9, 1900.

[74]See, for example, Charlotte *Observer,* Aug. 7, Aug. 10, 1900; Raleigh *Morning Post,* Aug 19, 1900.

[75]Connor, "A Saner Citizenship," Trinity College *Historical Papers,* ser. 4 (Durham, 1900), pp. 31-47.

[76]Connor to E. A. Alderman, Mar. 30, 1899, UNC Papers.

[77]Connor, p. 40.   [78]Nov. 17, Nov. 19, 1898.

[79]W. H. Page to Willia Alice Page, Feb. 17, 1899, Page Papers.

"has reached a point in industrial development where the business interests ought to assert their independence of prophet leadership and demand that our material interests must be considered every time."[80] In fact, the white supremacy victory considerably strengthened the position of men in the party, like Simmons and Aycock, who were anxious to encourage the rapid expansion of the state's economy. The new governor's dynamism and educational idealism contributed to his great personal popularity, but his laissez-faire inclinations and past associations with railroad interests were no doubt reassuring to businessmen.[81]

The support that many preachers gave to the white supremacy movement was probably more or less uncritical. They could see in its triumph a vindication of the rightful authority of the "superior" race, which they took for granted, but, quite as important, a vindication of the cause of religion, virtue, and all that southerners held sacred. For other denominational leaders, as for many businessmen, Democratic victory implied much more. Josiah Bailey had learned a valuable lesson from his political isolation in 1897. The defeat of local taxation that year was a sign of the weakness of Populist-Republican fusion and a portent of Democratic victory in 1898. The Democrats had hit upon a unifying issue, white supremacy. If churchmen like Bailey and Kilgo had ignored it, they could have found themselves isolated from rank-and-file Baptists and Methodists as well as from the resurgent Democracy. Hence, despite some misgivings, deriving particularly from their belief that the "incompetent" of both races should be disfranchised, they leaped aboard the white supremacy bandwagon. Party leaders like Simmons made things easier for them by seeking a compromise on the state aid issue. Even Daniels, giving Democratic victory first priority, went along with what Simmons had done.

From Daniels's point of view denominational leaders were supposed to be the mainstays of the old traditions and virtues, but from Bailey and Kilgo's point of view many of those traditions

---

[80]Quoted in Reidsville *Webster's Weekly*, Aug. 23, 1900.

[81]On Aycock's laissez-faire attitudes and probusiness bias, see Orr, pp. 89-90, 97, 100-101; Robert Watson Winston, *It's a Far Cry* (New York, 1937), pp. 253-54; and W. A. Graham to J. Bryan Grimes, Jan. 11, 1900, Grimes Papers, Southern Hist.Coll., UNC Lib.

and virtues were no longer relevant to the role that they believed the churches should play in making the New South a reality. They saw the victory of white supremacy as the final settlement of a troublesome issue, as the closing of one chapter in the South's history and the opening of another. Even before the August election Bailey expressed the hope that disfranchisement would result in "new parties and new leaders and new methods." After Aycock's victory, Bailey made several demands on the new administration, including more money for the public schools, free discussion of issues, fairer treatment of blacks, and the repudiation of "red shirt" campaign tactics.[82] The Baptist editor was hoping for a new consensus committed to the goal of progressive development with both unimaginative "mummies" and radical agrarians safely relegated to the past. In the euphoria of Democratic victory, the restoration of the old consensus of political, racial, and religious values was more apparent than real. Both the Clark-Kilgo affair and Bailey's deal with Simmons implied the development of a relationship between businessmen, politicians, and denominational leaders that would help secure the transition from an Old to a New Order in the body politic and in such key institutions as the churches. This alliance on the levels of both ideology and practical politics was not what Josephus Daniels had in mind when he invoked the aid of the old-time religion on behalf of white supremacy.

[82]*Biblical Recorder,* July 25, Aug. 8, 1900. See also ibid., Aug. 22, 1900.

VIII

From Racism to
"Business Progressivism"

THE PRAISE for Josiah Bailey that emanated from neopopulist Democrats during the white supremacy campaign was short-lived.[1] The fact that church leaders like Bailey and Kilgo had established close ties to the business community did not augur well for an end to denominational-political controversies. As soon as the racist demagoguery of 1898 and 1900 had served its purpose, businessmen and conservatives were anxious to see the race issue shelved as quickly as possible and a stable social order restored. Unfortunately, as Henry Groves Connor pointed out, "the politicians have stirred the minds and feelings of the people more deeply than they intended."[2] Strongly partisan, and often neopopulist, newspapers like the *News and Observer* and *Webster's Weekly* continued to agitate the "Negro question" although it presumably had been settled. Almost immediately after the state election in August 1900, Daniels began to cry that a vote for McKinley in November meant a vote for black officeholders in North Carolina.[3] Journals of business opinion, some of which were hoping for a McKinley victory, were quick to denounce such rhetoric as a betrayal of the understanding that race would cease to be an issue. The Charlotte *Observer* insisted that the "better element" of the Democracy opposed racism and accused the *News and Observer* of trying "to get up another red shirt campaign for November."[4] The *Morning Post* argued that Daniels's agitation "seriously disturbed" business.[5]

[1]Raleigh *News and Observer*, Aug. 16, 1898; Reidsville *Webster's Weekly*, Aug. 18, 1898.

[2]Connor to George Howard, Nov. 25, 1898, copy in the Connor Papers, Southern Hist. Coll., UNC Lib.

[3]Raleigh *News and Observer*, Aug. 12, Aug. 15, 1900. See also *Webster's Weekly*, Aug. 23, 1900.

[4]Sept. 4, Aug. 22, 1900. See also Aug. 11, Aug. 16, 1900.

[5]Aug. 16, 1900. See also Aug. 21, 1900.

Race had proved and would continue to prove a powerful weapon in the hands of such neopopulist Democratic leaders as Benjamin Tillman, James K. Vardaman, and Theodore Bilbo in other southern states, and North Carolina was not immune to it. Tarheel businessmen and "progressives" had used the race issue themselves in the very recent past, of course, but it no longer suited their purposes. It was hardly surprising that Bailey too was appalled at Daniels's persistence in keeping the race issue alive. Regarding it as a "breach of faith," the Baptist editor asked, "Shall we return to the bondage of blackness and passion from which we have just been delivered?"[6] In reply Daniels accused Bailey of political disloyalty and of being a Republican "at heart." He invoked the whole gamut of neopopulist concerns—the trusts, the gold standard, imperialism—to justify his continued use of the race issue in saving the state from Republicans and crypto-Republican Democrats.[7] In a letter to the *News and Observer* Bailey denied he was a Republican and claimed that he had received a personal pledge from Aycock and Simmons to abandon the politics of race.[8]

Daniels was not satisfied. He devoted the entire front page of his paper to demonstrate that the *Biblical Recorder* had been advocating "Republican doctrine."[9] Referring specifically to the *Biblical Recorder,* the *Morning Post,* and the Charlotte *Observer,* he declared that every editor "who is clamoring for 'a higher political plane' either bolted in 1896, is an anti-imperialist [sic], a gold bug, or a corporation organ."[10] He charged that those who advocated an end to the race issue were hypocrites. Daniels, who had earlier praised Bailey's participation in the white supremacy campaign, accused the Baptist editor of bringing politics into a religious paper.[11] "We rather object," added the Elizabeth City *Economist,* "to the youthful smart editor making the Biblical

[6]*Biblical Recorder,* Aug. 15, 1900.

[7]Raleigh *News and Observer,* Aug. 16, 1900.

[8]Aug. 17, 1900. The Charlotte *Observer,* Aug. 10, 1900, also reported that Simmons had pledged to abandon the race issue.

[9]Raleigh *News and Observer,* Aug. 19, 1900. See also ibid., Aug. 18, 1900.

[10]Ibid., Aug. 22, 1900. Daniels meant "imperialist."   [11]Ibid., Aug. 23, 1900.

Recorder a political engine, and prefer it to be, as it is, the expo-
nent and organ of Baptist principles."[12]

Bailey took to high moral ground to defend himself. The *News
and Observer,* he maintained, "wants to keep up Red Shirtism,
ballot-box frauds, suppression of free speech and general terror.
We do not."[13] Baptist Secretary White defended those preachers
who urged quiet on the racial front from the charge of meddling
in politics. "The proposition to continue agitation of the negro
issue . . . is more than a political question," he insisted.[14] However, in a front-page article in the *News and Observer,* Thomas M.
Hufham, son of a former editor of the *Recorder,* replied: "These
ministers of the Gospel and religious teachers are entitled to
respect for the goodness of their intentions and the purity of their
motives. . . . But absorbed in other work and devoted to other
interests they have failed to discern the face of the political
sky."[15] On the other hand, both the Charlotte *Observer* and the
Morning Post came to Bailey's defense. The Charlotte daily—which
during the war on the university had not hesitated to accuse Bailey
of "meddling in politics"—now called the *Biblical Recorder* the
"conscience of the State."[16]

The alignment of forces present in Bailey's dispute with Daniels
largely repeated itself in an important primary election campaign
in progress between Simmons and Julian S. Carr for the Democratic nomination to succeed to Marion Butler's seat in the United
States Senate. Although he was one of the wealthiest manufacturers in the state, Carr identified himself with the antitrust wing
of the Democracy, perhaps because he had been pushed out of the
tobacco business by the American Tobacco Company. Carr's
candidacy received the enthusiastic backing of *Webster's Weekly,*
but it forced Daniels into a position of neutrality. Simmons was
the party organization's candidate, but Carr was an old friend of
Daniels's, and had even lent him the money to purchase the *News
and Observer* in 1894. Both men, then, had claims on the editor's

[12]Quoted by ibid., Aug. 24, 1900.   [13]*Biblical Recorder,* Aug. 22, 1900.

[14]Quoted by ibid., Aug. 29, 1900. See also ibid., Sept. 5, Sept. 12, Oct. 3, Oct. 10,
1900.

[15]Sept. 2, 1900. See also Reidsville *Webster's Weekly,* Sept. 6, 1900.

[16]Charlotte *Observer,* Aug. 16, 1900. See also Raleigh *Morning Post,* Aug. 21, 1900.

loyalty.[17] Also, both men were Methodists. Simmons was a trustee of Trinity College, and Carr was a leading layman in the church. However, the state aid issue and Kilgo's close association with the Dukes had alienated Carr, an early benefactor of Trinity, from the college administration. Once, according to Webster, Kilgo went "white with rage" and ordered Carr's portrait removed from the college.[18] During a series of libel suits against Kilgo that grew out of the Clark controversy, "General Carr," according to Robert Winston, one of Kilgo's attorneys, "was putting up the funds, Chief Justice Clark was furnishing the law. Honorable Josephus Daniels and the Old Reliable [the *News and Observer*] were sowing the seeds of trust hatred."[19]

The senatorial contest again revealed how religious sentiment and denominational loyalty interacted with ideological and factional divisions in politics. Simmons recognized that Carr, because of his philanthropic endeavors and his "power in the Methodist Church," would quite likely draw considerable support from members of that denomination.[20] It was in fact forthcoming from Kilgo's enemies. Editor Crawford's *North Carolina Christian Advocate* broke the long-established practice of not taking part in partisan politics by joining Webster in firm support of Carr. Among the reasons the *Advocate* gave for backing him was his stand "with the people against Trusts and other forms of combined capital that oppress labor or monopolize the business of the country." When Thomas Ivey's Raleigh *Christian Advocate* criticized Crawford for meddling in politics, the latter replied that

[17] For an insistent defense of Carr as a silverite, Bryanite, and antimonopolist, see almost every issue of the Reidsville *Webster's Weekly* during Sept. and Oct. 1900. On Carr himself and his relations with Daniels, see Samuel A. Ashe, "Julian Shakespeare Carr," in *Biographical History of North Carolina,* ed. Samuel A. Ashe, 8 vols. (Greensboro, 1905-17), 2: 51-59; Josephus Daniels, *Tar Heel Editor* (Chapel Hill, 1939), p. 137; Daniels, *Editor in Politics* (Chapel Hill, 1941), pp. 85-88; and Daniels to his wife, Aug. 6, 1894, Daniels Papers, Ms. Div., Lib. Cong.

[18] John R. Webster to Raleigh *News and Observer*, Sept. 18, 1898. On Carr's relation to Trinity, see William Kenneth Boyd, "General Julian S. Carr and Trinity," *Trinity Alumni Register* 10 (1924): 252-55; Robert Lee Flowers to [?], [Nov. 1896], Josiah Bailey to J. C. Kilgo, July 27, 1898, Trinity College Papers, Duke Univ. Archives.

[19] Winston, *It's a Far Cry* (New York, 1937), p. 234.

[20] F. M. Simmons, *Statesman of the New South: Memoirs and Addresses,* ed. J. Fred Rippy (Durham, 1936), pp. 30-31.

partisanship was not involved since both Carr and Simmons belonged to the same party.[21] Carr did seek Kilgo's support, but he probably had few illusions about getting it. Bailey, in his correspondence with Kilgo, had long since classified "our benignant & beautiful Julian Carr" along with Daniels and Clark among "the sissys, the skunks, the demagogs and conspirators." During the senatorial primary campaign Bailey insisted to Kilgo that the two of them "in a quiet way" must set up a "counter movement" against Carr, especially since the latter "still counts on using the Methodist Church for himself." "These are critical times in N.C.," he continued, "and you and I must be more active than we would otherwise be. Every inch of ground counts."[22]

Simmons won the election quite handily. Kilgo received word that Simmons appreciated "the efforts of none more than those of the faculty of Trinity College."[23] But in its analysis of Carr's defeat, *Webster's Weekly* took Bailey and Kilgo severely to task for their role in the campaign, especially for criticisms that they had made of Crawford's political use of the *Advocate*. Bailey, Webster charged, "talks more politics to his readers in one week than Dr. Crawford writes for the North Carolina Christian Advocate in a year. . . . Bailey and Kilgo protesting against mixing Church and State is one of the rich things of the year."[24] Yet Crawford's days as editor were numbered. In 1901 he attacked Trinity for "leaving at a great distance the old landmarks, set by our doctrinal standards . . . , under the guise of freedom of thought."[25] After Kilgo replied by accusing Crawford of attempting "to poison the minds" of Methodists, the editor's son physically assaulted the college president on board a train.[26] "While I regret the difficulty," the textile manufacturer W. R. Odell stated to Kilgo, "it is going to bring the issue of the Advocate before the Western North Carolina Conference, and this is what I want." "I feel like the war

[21]*North Carolina Christian Advocate*, Sept. 12, Oct. 10, 1900.

[22]Carr to Kilgo, Sept. 13, 1900, Bailey to Kilgo, Nov. 9, 1897, Sept. 10, 1900, Trinity College Papers.

[23]T. B. Womack to Kilgo, Nov. 12, 1900, ibid.   [24]Nov. 15, 1900.

[25]*North Carolina Christian Advocate*, June 26, 1901. See also ibid., May 15, 1901.

[26]W. W. Duncan to Kilgo, July 26, 1901, James Southgate to Kilgo, Aug. 9, 1901, Kilgo Papers, Duke Univ. Archives; and Paul Neff Garber, *John Carlisle Kilgo, President of Trinity College, 1894-1910* (Durham, 1937), pp. 236-37.

is nearly over," added the banker Joseph G. Brown.[27] Crawford's dark warnings about "outside influences" interfering in the affairs of the western conference proved of no avail. At the conference meeting in November, he "retired." Bailey remarked triumphantly to Kilgo, "I am glad that Crawford is dead and buried. It is a good sign in the Almanac for the Methodists."[28]

Carr and Crawford had been defeated, but Kilgo was to encounter a more serious challenge to his efforts to provide ideological leadership for North Carolina Methodism. The race issue was still potent, and in 1903 it threatened to undermine the relationship between denominational leaders and the new political order. In the fall of that year John Spencer Bassett, professor of history at Trinity, wrote an essay exposing what he perceived to be a serious threat to progress and stability. It appeared under the title "Stirring Up the Fires of Race Antipathy" in the October issue of the *South Atlantic Quarterly,* a journal recently launched at the college and expressive of the enlightened scholarship that the Methodist institution was trying to promote.[29] The event that provided the immediate occasion for the essay was the *News and Observer's* vitriolic reaction to the fact that while traveling by train through the state in August, Booker T. Washington and a large party of black people were allowed to use the main dining room in a hotel in the town of Hamlet.[30] Bassett used this incident as an example of the political manipulation of racial animosities. Many of the same Democrats who had promised that disfranchisement would usher in a utopia of racial peace and high-minded politics, he complained, continued to play upon the race issue for partisan purposes. "A certain emotional and 'yellow' newspaper"—clearly the *News and Observer*—"was conspicuous in its lurid descriptions." Bassett then suggested that Washington was "the greatest man, save General Lee, born in the South in a hundred years" and predicted that black people "will win equality at some time."

On November 1 the *News and Observer* replied with banner headlines reading, "PROF. BASSETT SAYS NEGRO WILL WIN EQUALITY."

[27]Odell to Kilgo, July 23, 1901, Brown to Kilgo, July 30, 1901, Trinity College Papers.

[28]*North Carolina Christian Advocate,* Oct. 23, Oct. 30, Nov. 27, 1901; Bailey to Kilgo, Dec. 1, 1901, Trinity College Papers.

[29]2 (1903): 297-305.   [30]Aug. 25, 1903.

Daniels characterized the Trinity professor as a "freak" who was attempting "to create contempt for Southern traditions and . . . to revolutionize Southern political convictions." Bassett's challenge to racial politics caused much of the North Carolina press, led by the *News and Observer,* to agitate for his removal, and President Kilgo's to boot, from the college.[31] During the ensuing controversy academic freedom became an issue, but the *News and Observer's* stand did not violate that principle, according to Daniels, because there "are some questions that are settled and not open to discussion. In the South one of them is that the Anglo-Saxon race is superior to the Negro race." Bassett showed not only a "hostility to the old-time creeds and traditions" of the South, but to make matters worse, he was "feeding on the husks of trust contempt for the rights of the people." Claiming to speak for "the great majority of Methodists," the *News and Observer* published an interview with a certain "prominent Methodist" of the eastern conference who reported deep dissatisfaction in the denomination with "the spirit of materialism and commercialism that seems to be the very life and breath of the college." Bassett was simply the last straw. Kilgo, the Methodist said, was "strenuous in his talk about breadth and liberality and that sort of thing, except about trusts and illegal combinations to rob tobacco farmers."[32] For good measure, *Webster's Weekly* added that every professor at Trinity, save two, was a "free thinker."[33] Trinity College, once "dear to the hearts of old-fashioned Methodists," had become "alien to North Carolina Methodism and North Carolina policies," Daniels concluded.[34]

Bassett's essay contained rhetoric which, as he told Walter Hines Page, was calculated to shock people, "to wake them up."[35] But actually he added little of substance to a relatively enlightened

[31]The most important secondary accounts of the Bassett affair are Garber, pp. 239-86; Richard Hofstadter and Walter P. Metzger, *The Development of Academic Freedom in the United States* (New York, 1955), pp. 171-76; and Earl W. Porter, *Trinity and Duke, 1892-1924: Foundations of Duke University* (Durham, 1964), pp. 96-139. For a qualified defense of Daniels, see Joseph L. Morrison, *Josephus Daniels Says . . . : An Editor's Political Odyssey from Bryan to Wilson and F.D.R., 1894-1913* (Chapel Hill, 1962), pp. 123-47.

[32]Nov. 19, Nov. 20, Nov. 15, 1903. See also Dec. 3, Nov. 10, 1903.

[33]Nov. 5, 1903. See also Nov. 15, 1903.

[34]Raleigh *News and Observer,* Dec. 17, 1903.

[35]Bassett to Page, Dec. 14, 1903, Page Papers, Houghton Lib., Harvard Univ.

view of the race issue that Kilgo had already adopted. In 1896 Kilgo had invited Washington to appear for the first time on the campus of a white college in the South.[36] In an article in the *Biblical Recorder* in 1901 Kilgo had maintained that denial of suffrage to the blacks imposed a "greater duty" on the state to prepare the disfranchised for their obligations as citizens in the future. "'It is my duty to get you ready to vote,'" he had stated, "and this it [the state] will say unless partizanship has buried statesmanship, and state existence has passed into party existence."[37] In the same issue of the *South Atlantic Quarterly* in which Bassett's article appeared, Kilgo argued that the black man's weaknesses are failings common to all men "regardless of racial distinction." He strongly condemned such popular racist tracts as Thomas Dixon's novel *The Leopard's Spots.* Finally, Kilgo denied that "industrial education" alone did justice to the black man's potential. The latter's right to a "full education" rested "upon the right of every man to look as far into the universe as he can."[38]

Bassett's views, then, were by no means idiosyncratic at Trinity, if not in the state as a whole. The Bassett affair became a *cause célèbre* for those who saw themselves in the vanguard of the battle against southern traditionalism. Page, who took a keen interest in the progress of the controversy, corresponded regularly during the late fall and winter with members of the Trinity community to bolster their morale. He told Ben Duke that Daniels's attack provided "the best chance that ever came or that ever could come for Trinity to show that it is the home of free thought and free speech." "If these fools," he went on, "who now howl and demand Basset's dismissal are allowed to have their own way, what will be the result? They will think that they own the state."[39] Kilgo, the college faculty, and the Dukes themselves refused to be intimidated and backed Bassett to the hilt. The college board of trustees, meeting on December 1, heeded Page's advice and voted

---

[36]Porter, p. 108.   [37]Nov. 13, 1901.

[38]Kilgo, "Our Duty to the Negro," *South Atlantic Quarterly* 2 (1903): 369-85. Kilgo maintained excellent relations with Shaw University, a black college in Raleigh (see Nathaniel Bruce to Kilgo, June 10, 1899, Josiah Bailey to Kilgo, Dec. 22, 1900, Trinity College Papers).

[39]Page to Duke, Thanksgiving Day, 1903, copy in the Page Papers. See also Edwin Mims to Page, Nov. 24, 1903, Bassett to Page, Nov. 7, Dec. 3, Dec. 8, Dec. 14, 1903, ibid.

eighteen to seven to retain Bassett. In a stirring affirmation of academic freedom, the trustees declared their opposition "to any coercion of thought." "A reasonable freedom of opinion," the board concluded, "is to a college the very breath of life." An ecstatic Page told Professor William Preston Few that "the victory added about ten years to my life."[40]

Despite Bassett's vindication by the trustees, Kilgo's ability to impress his point of view on the Methodist church seemed badly shaken. Methodist opposition to Bassett was considerable. Even Kilgo's old supporter, editor Ivey of the Raleigh *Christian Advocate,* voted as a trustee for Bassett's dismissal. He defended his action as "necessary to the welfare of Trinity College, the property of North Carolina Methodism, and to those social interests in North Carolina which are as fundamental and sacred as those of free speech and academic liberty."[41] The *North Carolina Christian Advocate,* now edited by a man friendly to Trinity, the Reverend H. M. Blair, counseled silence on the race problem to avoid "playing with fire." It regretted the board's decision not to dismiss Bassett.[42] The clergymen who spoke at the meeting of the trustees, according to a Trinity student, seemed "badly frightened by the popular clamor." One preacher "begged" his fellow trustees to fire Bassett, for if they did not do so, he would "not dare go back to his congregation."[43]

Page saw the whole episode as confirmation of his own progressive critique of southern politics and religion. Page's *World's Work,* while lambasting the political motives that prompted Daniels's attack on Bassett, showed that the principal source of opposition to the professor came from "the church element" of the board. "Political and religious forces," it concluded, "as a rule are reactionary. . . . The political and religious life lags even when it does

---

[40]"Trinity College and Academic Liberty," *South Atlantic Quarterly* 3 (1904): 62-64; Page to Few, Dec. 8, 1903, copy in the Page Papers.

[41]Dec. 9, 1903.

[42]Nov. 4, Dec. 9, 1903. For the anti-Bassett stand of one Methodist congregation, see "Resolution Passed by the M.E. Church of Smithfield, N.C., in Regard to Prof. John Spencer Bassett of Trinity College," Nov. 11, 1903, typescript in the Trinity College Papers.

[43]E. C. Perrow, "Trinity College, N.C., and Academic Freedom," 1958, typescript in the Trinity College Papers. Perrow's statement is based on a diary he kept while a student at Trinity in 1903.

not drag."[44] William Garrott Brown offered an analysis similar to
Page's. He was in Durham at the time and even helped draft a
statement which the Trinity faculty presented to the trustees on
Bassett's behalf.[45] He reported to a northern newspaper that the
politicians "knew admirably how to use" an influential but easily
manipulated class, the clergy. "The Methodist preachers," he
asserted, "are the preservers of every old idea. Timid to the point
of cowardice, they can be driven to any cruel action if they are
made to think that the pillars of society are about to be pulled
down."[46] The analysis of Page and Brown stood in stark contrast
to the statement of the trustees that their decision was made with
a "due regard" for the "spirit and doctrines" of a "tolerant and
generous" Methodism.[47]

In his efforts to rally "old-fashioned" Methodists against
Trinity, Daniels appeared to be playing the kind of nonproductive,
indeed regressive, politics that men like Page and Brown detested.
Daniels had once been a close friend of Page's, but as the latter became increasingly critical of certain features of southern life, their
friendship waned. "I did not sympathize with his strictures,"
Daniels later recalled.[48] In November 1903 the *News and Observer*
printed on its front page in bold type a letter from former North
Carolina Congressman Wharton J. Green severely denouncing Page
for treason against the South comparable to Bassett's. He accused
Page of deserting "his country" and making "a vile diatribe against
the women of his native land, its clergy, and its public men." Not
neglecting Brown, the *News and Observer* called his analysis of the

[44]7 (1904): 4284-87.

[45]*The Papers and Addresses of William Preston Few*, ed. Robert H. Woody (Durham, 1951), p. 42.

[46]Boston *Evening Transcript*, Dec. 9, 1903. The author of this article was "a special correspondent of the Transcript" who purported to offer the "inside Story," and cer-tainly it was written by someone who was well acquainted with people at the college. Brown began a series of articles on the South in the *Transcript* beginning in February under the pseudonym "Stanton." Since Brown was in Durham at the time of the earlier article, it is reasonable to assume that he wrote it. See also the essay on Brown, which discusses the "Stanton" articles, in Wendell Holmes Stephenson, *Southern History in the Making: Pioneer Historians of the South* (Baton Rouge, La., 1964), pp. 27-51.

[47]"Trinity College and Academic Liberty," *South Atlantic Quarterly* 3 (1904): 64.

[48]Daniels, *Tar Heel Editor*, p. 256. See also ibid., p. 272; Burton J. Hendrick, *The Life and Letters of Walter H. Page*, 2 vols. (Garden City and New York, 1923), 1: 119-20; Daniels to Page, Oct. 16, 1896, Page Papers.

Bassett affair "cruel slander," "inspired by a spirit that has grown up at Trinity College" where, among other things, preachers "who deny the fundamental doctrines of the Methodist Church" were allowed to give sermons.[49]

Daniels's reputation as an archetypal southern progressive—a Bryanite, a Wilsonian, a mentor of Franklin D. Roosevelt—has made his attack on Trinity difficult for some to fathom. Wilbur J. Cash, for example, could only believe that Daniels, "one of the most liberal and intelligent editors the South has had," had simply been "swept into the current," presumably against his own better judgment. Professor Few, however, denied the legitimacy of Daniels's reputation and dismissed him as one "distinguished for his supposed liberalism." Bassett explained to Charles Francis Adams that Daniels had been trying for some time to arouse popular opposition against Kilgo by showing that Trinity was an alien influence in the South.[50]

Daniels did have personal grievances against Kilgo that went back to the war on the university; he identified himself with that wing in the Methodist church which opposed the policies of Trinity's president. As a leading figure in the Democratic party, he no doubt felt that Bassett's essay was subversive of the racial and political settlement of 1900. Moreover, Daniels's hostility to the large corporations led him to oppose the considerable influence that men connected with the American Tobacco Company had in the affairs of the college and the Methodist church. But fundamentally Daniels was out of touch with those groups in the state who believed that traditionalism in politics, religion, and race was a barrier to progress, who had faith in the progressive impact of industrialization and dynamic capitalism, and who wanted the region to swim in the main currents of national life. Bassett, for example, praised "the force of industrialism" for "changing the whole intellectual outlook of the people."[51] Trinity represented those forces that men like Daniels were not yet ready to accept.[52] Daniels could sound radical enough when he criticized the

[49]Nov. 24, Dec. 27, 1903.

[50]Cash, *The Mind of the South* (New York, 1941), p. 331; *Papers and Addresses of Few*, p. 34; Bassett to Adams, Nov. 3, 1911, photostat copy in the Bassett Papers, Duke Univ. Archives (original in private possession).

[51]Bassett, "How Industrialism Builds Up Education," *World's Work* 8 (1904): 5030.

[52]Edwin Mims to Page, Nov. 24, 1903, Page Papers.

"interests," but actually he, along with other neopopulists, possessed a vision of society that harked back to a more traditional community before the economic changes of the late nineteenth century had made their impact. His opposition to monopolies and his solicitude for the people were thus not inconsistent with a traditional religious and racial point of view.

The most consistent supporters of Bassett on the board of trustees were those whom the *World's Work* praised as "men of affairs . . . the men who do things . . . the men who are moving forward."[53] Of the seven men who voted against Bassett, five were preachers, one was a businessman, and one, a politician, Senator Simmons. On Bassett's side stood four preachers and eleven business or professional men.[54] Simmons's position was perhaps a difficult one. He had had excellent relations with Kilgo; but Bassett's attack on the white supremacy movement, which Simmons had masterminded, gave the senator little choice in the matter—especially after Daniels had stirred up public opinion against the professor and the college. Simmons was a politician, and since Page's best of all possible worlds without politicians had not yet arrived, he had to behave like one. Indeed, he may have regarded Bassett's article, and not only Daniels's predictable response, as upsetting to the racial peace. John Webster, no friend of the senator's, believed that the preservation of "the fruits of the great victory of 1900" demanded that Simmons "draw the line against Kilgoism and Bassettism" by resigning from the board.[55] It was significant that Simmons remained a trustee until 1910.

The Raleigh *Morning Post* and the Charlotte *Observer* found Bassett's article discomforting; but, unlike Senator Simmons, who had to think of his own political future, they could afford to defend the professor out of broader ideological considerations. At first the *Morning Post* described Bassett's essay as "astonishing and painful"; but as the issues became clearer, it modified its position. The paper accepted Bassett's explanation that he was not advocating "social equality" and urged "fair play" toward the professor. It ended up by praising the Trinity board for not accepting Bassett's resignation and Kilgo for not allowing the college and the

[53]"A Notable Victory for Academic Freedom," *World's Work* 7 (1904): 4287.

[54]Raleigh *News and Observer*, Dec. 3, 1903; Porter, p. 133.

[55]Reidsville *Webster's Weekly*, Dec. 3, 1903.

church to become "the instruments of schemers and demagogues, political and otherwise."[56] Daniels, who called the *Morning Post* "the organ of Bassettism as well as of the Southern Railway and the Cigarette Trust," assumed that the paper changed its line after it "GOT ITS ORDERS ."[57]

Long before the Bassett affair editor Caldwell of the Charlotte *Observer* realized that in Kilgo he had an ally against that wing of the Democracy for which Daniels spoke. "I quite agree with you," Caldwell told Kilgo in 1901, "that the time has come in North Carolina when freedom must be made free; or if one may not differ with Mr. Daniels except at the sacrifice of his character it is time we were finding it out." The paper considered Bassett's essay "unfortunate and harmful" but insisted that the professor ought to be able to express his views in complete freedom.[58] Both Bassett and Kilgo were satisfied with the *Observer'*s position. Caldwell appreciated Kilgo's "commendation of the general policy" of the paper and added, "I am really and honestly trying to do something to promote higher and better thought in North Carolina and the South."[59]

Josiah Bailey also defended Bassett's right to speak. The *Biblical Recorder* regretted some of his utterances but unequivocally denounced the attacks on him. "The average reader," it insisted, "has utterly lost sight of the fact that the Professor's article was not an argument for equality, but a protest from the historian's point of view against the use of race antipathy as a political issue."[60] Bailey's support did not go unappreciated. "He means much to us," Bassett told Page. Bailey's position was fully consistent with his commitment to "progress"; he shared Page's vision and said so in the *Biblical Recorder* when other newspapers accused the former Tarheel of disloyalty to southern institutions.[61] Bailey wrote to Page commending his efforts against the South's "poverty and isolation" and praising "the force of the new

---

[56]Nov. 3, Nov. 8, Dec. 1, Dec. 3, 1903.

[57]Raleigh *News and Observer*, Dec. 16, 1903.

[58]Caldwell to Kilgo, Dec. 18, 1901, Trinity College Papers; Charlotte *Observer*, Nov. 9, 1903. See also ibid., Nov. 30, Dec. 3, 1903.

[59]Caldwell to Kilgo, Nov. 11, 1903, Trinity College Papers.

[60]Nov. 18, 1903. See also Oct. 28, Nov. 4, Dec. 9, 1903.

[61]Bassett to Page, Dec. 8, 1903, Page Papers; *Biblical Recorder*, July 3, 1901.

movement that is giving you and me joy." He could only lament
to Page during the Bassett controversy that the "brethren all think
that they are free." For Daniels the Baptist editor had nothing but
ridicule: "It is really ludicrous to think that the man essays to be
Lord High Censor of all of North Carolina."[62]

It so happened that Bailey and a Baptist preacher, Jasper C.
Massee, came under fire from the *News and Observer* at the same
time that Daniels was waging war on Bassett—and largely for the
same reasons. Almost two months before Bassett published his
essay, the *News and Observer* reported that Massee, the minister at
the Baptist Tabernacle in Raleigh, had warned in a sermon that
"blood will run in the streets" unless blacks received justice at the
hands of white southerners. The preacher demanded that "the black
man should be treated as a human being." Daniels accused Massee
of inciting "vicious negroes to unreasonable and impossible demands." In return, at the Baptist convention in December, Massee
proclaimed that "the day will come when the license of the editors
of our great daily papers will have to be curtailed" and went on to
say that a great burden had been put on the religious press to
interpret the race problem fairly. Daniels, recoiling at this denial
of freedom of the press, compared Massee to the infamous Bassett
and insisted that neither man represented the attitude of the
Baptist and Methodist churches. Moreover, the Raleigh editor detected a conspiracy. Massee and Bassett were the tools of certain
"malignant religio-political bosses . . . aided by all the trusts and
monopolies in the State" whose real purpose it was to destroy the
News and Observer.[63] Bailey responded to Daniels's outburst with
a long letter to the Charlotte *Observer* and the *Morning Post.* He
accused Daniels of "hectoring the religious denominations." The
News and Observer's violent journalism, Bailey charged, drove
"some of the best men in the commonwealth out of the [Demo-
cratic] party's councils."[64]

Daniels returned to the offensive by resurrecting the arguments
that he had used against Bailey in their dispute in 1900 over the

[62]Bailey to Page, July 30, 1902, Dec. 23, 1903, Page Papers.

[63]Raleigh *News and Observer,* Sept. 5, Dec. 13, Dec. 15, Dec. 16, 1903. Massee, a
native of Georgia, was a minister in Raleigh from 1903 to 1908. He was a well-known
evangelist at Boston's Tremont Temple after 1922.

[64]Bailey to the Charlotte *Observer,* Dec. 19, 1903; Bailey to the Raleigh *Morning
Post,* Dec. 20, 1903.

race issue in politics. Bailey's animosity toward the *News and Observer*, Daniels insisted, was "political and is based on nothing but politics." The *Biblical Recorder* preached "Republican doctrine" instead of spiritual religion and was a spokesman for "the Southern Railway, Cigarette Trust, Whiskey Ring, and the Kilgo-Bassett crowd." Methodists, he claimed, resented Bailey's intrusion into their affairs during the Bassett controversy. Moreover, the *Biblical Recorder* was beginning "to upset the political faith of a few life-long Democratic Baptists." Daniels found it interesting that Bailey should have chosen to publish his letter in the Charlotte *Observer*, "the Hanna and Whiskey organ of North Carolina," which had failed to support Bryan in 1900. Bailey and Caldwell of the *Observer* had been extremely critical of each other during the state aid controversy, as Daniels now gleefully pointed out, but they had since become "political Siamese twins" and enemies of the *News and Observer*'s "uncompromising Democracy."[65] However, the *Observer,* as well as the *Morning Post,* was contemptuous of Daniels's attack on Massee and Bailey. Noting the "fervid" and unanimous endorsement of Bailey's editorship at the Baptist convention, the Charlotte paper praised him as "incisive" and "independent."[66]

Bailey's ability to continue to find favor among Tarheel Baptists assembled in convention had significant parallels in the Methodist church. The initial fearful reaction of Methodist ministers to the Bassett affair raised the possibility that the professor's vindication by the board of trustees would become a Pyrrhic victory both for him and Kilgo. But Daniels's attempt to invoke the shibboleths of racial and religious solidarity did not work in the last analysis. At the height of the controversy Daniels could but marvel at Kilgo's ability to prevent the Bassett affair from even being discussed at the two Methodist conferences.[67] Preachers may have been a timid lot, but their first loyalty, in most cases, was to their church and its institutions. It is quite likely that the very ferocity of Daniels's attack caused many churchmen to rally to the support of Trinity

[65] Raleigh *News and Observer*, Dec. 24, 1903. For examples of Caldwell and Bailey's earlier hostility, see ibid., July 30, 1897; Charlotte *Observer*, July 24, Aug. 5, 1897; *Biblical Recorder*, Aug. 4, 1897.

[66] Charlotte *Observer*, Dec. 14, 1903. See also Raleigh *Morning Post*, Dec. 17, 1903.

[67] Raleigh *News and Observer*, Nov. 24, Nov. 29, Dec. 1, 1903. See also Reidsville *Webster's Weekly*, Nov. 9, 1903.

and its president, as they had during the Clark controversy. Despite his opposition to Bassett, Thomas Ivey deplored the "evident attempt" of "certain" newspapers to divert attention from the main issue, Bassett's article, in order to attack Kilgo and the college.[68] Although he had urged Bassett to resign, the Reverend Mr. Blair of the *North Carolina Christian Advocate* noted that "the recent frenzy, led by Mr. Daniels, surprises and pains many of his former friends."[69] Perhaps some preachers changed their minds when it became clearer which side it was more expedient to support. After the trustees had acted, a Methodist minister at Statesville who had opposed Bassett suddenly saw the light and announced his unequivocal support for the professor.[70]

The success of Bailey and Kilgo in maintaining their positions in the face of Daniels's attacks did not mean that racial prejudice among Tarheel Protestants was any less intense in 1903 than in 1898 or 1900 when the Democrats had exploited it so successfully. Nor did it mean greater justice for black people. For example, in the area of schools, on which Bailey placed so much emphasis, "the Aycock era was one of rapid deterioration in the concept of universal education, and of retrogression in the actual facilities provided for Negro schoolchildren."[71] Daniels's failure did mean that important elements in the Democratic party and especially in the business community intended to do everything in their power to prevent the politics of race from undermining the stability that the victory of 1900 had promised. They were even prepared to tolerate the outbursts, ill-advised though they seemed, of a Bassett or Massee. Indeed, such toleration was a hallmark of the liberal and progressive society they believed they were creating. Bailey and Kilgo, among denominational leaders, were seeking to reorient the power of traditional religion on behalf of this new society. They found their allies among businessmen and those who had faith in the promise of capitalist development. This alliance manifested itself during the Clark controversy, was strengthened by Bailey's deal with Simmons, and was confirmed during the Bassett affair.

[68]Raleigh *Christian Advocate*, Nov. 18, 1903.   [69]Dec. 25, 1903.

[70]H. K. Boyer to James H. Southgate, Nov. 21, 1903, Jan. 12, 1904, Trinity College Papers.

[71]Louis R. Harlan, *Separate and Unequal: Public School Campaigns and Racism in the Southern Seaboard States, 1901-1905* (paperback ed., New York, 1968), p. 110.

Churchmen like Bailey and˙Kilgo were promulgating a social gospel for the New South. They embraced the secular goals of capitalist development, but at the same time they sought to preserve the authority of the churches in a changing society. The war on the university revealed the tension in their thinking. The churches traditionally exercised their authority in the spiritual and moral realm, and doubtless many opponents of the university believed that secular education would dangerously undermine the influence of religion in molding people's lives. Kilgo's commitment to "Christian education" reflected, at least rhetorically, this kind of concern; yet as many of his critics recognized, his policies at Trinity had less to do with the traditional concerns of Methodism than with the secular values of New South capitalism. At Trinity, Kilgo was laying the foundations for Duke University, whose later development was indistinguishable from that of other institutions of higher education in modern American society. Ironically, for some of Kilgo's opponents, like Theodore Kingsbury, the university seemed to be more representative of the traditions of the Old Order that Trinity had forsaken. The university itself, of course, was about to embark on a period of rapid expansion which would make it a center for critical investigations of southern society. The denominational crusade for public schools also appeared to contradict the original purpose of the war on the university. Charles Taylor's rather artificial distinction between "secular" elementary education and "Christian" higher education amounted, whether he realized it or not, to a capitulation before the forces of secularization. If one accepted the assumptions of New South advocates that education at all levels was essential to progress, and Bailey and Kilgo certainly did, then the distinction became even less relevant.

In any case, the state aid issue drifted into oblivion after the turn of the century. Although late in 1900 Bailey assured Kilgo that "our fighting has only begun," neither man played a very active role in attempting to limit appropriations during the legislative session of 1901.[72] It was clear that by 1900 the establishment of a "sane" and progressive business-oriented administration in North Carolina was of more importance to Bailey and Kilgo than keeping up the old battle. Major spokesmen of the New Order, such as

[72]Bailey to Kilgo, Dec. 22, 1900, Trinity College Papers.

Tompkins and Caldwell of the Charlotte *Observer,* were deeply committed to state-supported higher education. Bailey and Kilgo must have known that despite the temporary victory that the deal with Simmons gave them, they were waging a losing war. Moreover, the end of the depression and the gifts of wealthy donors to the church colleges made the problem of competition less acute. By 1902 Bailey had decided (so he informed Kilgo) to devote his energies "on the inside now . . . to straighten up Wake Forest." In a revealing letter to John White, Bailey expressed regret that he had ever become involved in the state aid fracas. He blamed everything on his own youth and the blandishments of Columbus Durham and Charles Taylor. "I cannot believe in the fight I have made," he wearily concluded. The *Biblical Recorder* could now assure its readers that state higher education was neither godless nor evil. For Bailey at least the tension had been resolved in favor of secularization.[73] In 1903 the state convention simply asked Baptists to support their own colleges.[74]

For a critic of the churches like Walter Hines Page these developments must have been encouraging. He was convinced that Protestantism had been a retrograde force in southern society, supporting old attitudes and values that inhibited the triumph of an energetic capitalism. The appeal that Josephus Daniels made during the Bassett affair to racial animosity and "old-fashioned" Methodism was a case in point. But the Populists had shown that by the 1890s preachers were already beginning to adjust to a new reality. They retained much of the old vocabulary and forms but were prepared, implicitly at least, to accept the hegemony of a rising business class. Indeed, some preachers embraced the New South gospel wholeheartedly; and Bailey and Kilgo, rejecting the old doctrine of the spiritual nature of the church, wanted to teach preachers a new language altogether. While Populist critics realized that old forms could belie new commitments, men like Daniels clung obstinately to the forms themselves, as if these could provide a bulwark against unsettling social changes. Daniels shared many Populist concerns but often lost sight of them in the murky

[73]Bailey to Kilgo, June 26, 1902, ibid.; Bailey to John [White], July 17, 1902, Bailey Papers, Duke Univ. Lib.; *Biblical Recorder,* Feb. 26, 1902.

[74]*Minutes of the Annual Meeting of the Baptist State Convention of North Carolina . . . 1903,* p. 69.

waters of racism and traditionalism. In their own ways both Page and the Populists recognized the mechanisms of hegemony whereby cultural, religious, and institutional forces combine to sustain a particular complex of economic, social, and political power. Since the collapse of the slave regime that complex was changing, and the Populist revolt was a crucial stage in the process. The Populists, although perceptive in much of their criticism and able to draw on genuine popular discontent and much that was vital in popular culture, including evangelical Protestantism, failed to provide a consistent ideological alternative. At least in the churches the New South gospel proved too potent a competitor. It had powerful evangelical appeal. In practice it was not inconsistent with traditional spiritual concerns. And it was sustained by businessmen who gave generously of their wealth.

In this respect the Populists were more perceptive than Page. They realized that the triumph of New South capitalism did not require all, or even most, preachers to shed completely the homespun of traditionalism for the new fashions of progress. New South ideologues committed to economic development considered themselves the progressives, but at the same time they were building a society in which the vested interests of businessmen were paramount, and those interests often required a conservative defense. North Carolina's "business progressive" administrations in the 1920s had no use for labor unions and often supplied businessmen with the services of the state militia, most notably at Gastonia in 1929. At that particular strike, millowners could "fall back upon paternalism and the timeworn cries of religion and individualism" in fighting the union.[75] One imagines that Bailey and Kilgo would have approved these tactics. For they differed most markedly from Page in believing that the churches' role in preserving the cohesion and stability of the community was fundamental. The process of social change is always beset with contradictions, and new ideologies absorb and transform older values. The preaching of a New South gospel did not completely muffle the "timeworn cries of religion," and both would strengthen the hegemony of North Carolina's "Progressive Plutocracy."

[75] George B. Tindall, *The Emergence of the New South, 1913-1945* (Baton Rouge, La., 1967), p. 351. For an analysis of the continued potency of traditional religion at Gastonia, see Liston Pope, *Millhands and Preachers: A Study of Gastonia* (New Haven, 1949).

Essay on Manuscript Sources
Index

Essay on Manuscript Sources

The manuscript sources for this period of North Carolina history are immense. Apart from the papers of major figures in this study, useful items can turn up in almost any collection covering the 1890s.

The most important depository of manuscripts relating to North Carolina history is the Southern Historical Collection of the University of North Carolina Library at Chapel Hill. The Marion Butler Papers are the best single source for Populist politics. Another collection of papers of a Populist leader is that of Cyrus Thompson, which has some material on his attack on the churches. The Henry Groves Connor Papers were useful in revealing the thoughts of a Democratic conservative. The papers of Augustus W. Graham, Walter Clark's brother-in-law, shed light on the Clark-Kilgo controversy and on political matters in general. In the Robert W. Winston Papers, otherwise thin for the 1890s, there is an interesting manuscript analysis of the Clark-Kilgo controversy. The Daniel A. Tompkins Papers have much valuable material on industrial development in North Carolina. The Julian S. Carr Papers and the Theodore Bryant Kingsbury Papers, which should have proved helpful, were disappointingly thin. The following collections yielded at most an occasional useful item: the James Atkins Papers, the Alexander D. Betts Papers, the H. E. C. Bryant Papers, the Armistead Burwell Papers, the Bennehan Cameron Papers, the Heriot Clarkson Papers, the Charles L. Coon Papers, the Charles W. Dabney Papers, the J. Bryan Grimes Papers, the John Steele Henderson Papers, the Richmond Pearson Papers, the Thomas M. Pittman Papers, the Matt W. Ransom Papers, the Thomas Settle Papers, the Simpson-Bryan Papers, and the Francis Winston Papers. In the University Archives the papers of the University of North Carolina proved to be quite helpful in revealing the strategy of university officials during the state aid fights of 1895 and 1897. In addition, President Edwin A. Alderman's correspondence with party leaders throughout the state provided insight into the complex political problems of the 1890s.

The Duke University Archives in Durham, North Carolina, contain the most important single manuscript source for this study, the voluminous Trinity College Papers. Most of John C. Kilgo's incoming correspondence while he was president of Trinity is to be found here. The collection reflects his many interests, which were not confined to the college but extended to the Methodist church, politics, and education in general. The John C. Kilgo Papers contain some correspondence for the 1890s but consist mostly of manuscript sermons and addresses. The William Garrott Brown Papers were of some value but more interesting was a recently discovered box of his letters to William Preston Few now located in the papers of the latter. The Herbert Baxter Adams Papers and the John Spencer Bassett Papers are partial collections consisting of photostats from, respectively, the Johns Hopkins University Library and private sources. A few useful items were found in the William Kenneth Boyd Papers.

In the Duke University Library were some collections of value. The Benjamin N. Duke Papers not only deal with the business activities of the Dukes but reveal their deep concern with the affairs of North Carolina Methodism. The William L. Grissom Papers contain some useful information on the problems of the Methodist press. Most of the material in the James Southgate Papers concerning the Clark-Kilgo controversy has been published elsewhere. Unfortunately the Josiah W. Bailey Papers contain almost nothing of importance before the second decade of the twentieth century apart from an intriguing letter to John E. White. Much the same can be said for the Furnifold M. Simmons Papers. Other collections in the Duke Library, the investigation of which turned up few tangible results, are the Marmaduke Hawkins Papers, the Samuel F. Patterson Papers, the Thomas J. Taylor Papers, and the William C. Tyree Papers.

The collections of the North Carolina State Archives proved less valuable in part because much of the material there relevant to this study has been published. This is true of both the Walter Clark Papers and the Cornelia Phillips Spencer Papers. The Papers of the Superintendent of Public Instruction, however, contain a vast amount of material on the public schools and shed light on the activities of Charles Mebane. Of little value were the William H. Burgwyn Papers and the Benjamin Rice Lacy Papers.

An important source was the Charles D. McIver Papers in the library of the University of North Carolina at Greensboro. The papers reflect the important role McIver played in the battles over state aid and the public schools. They also contain important letters dealing with both education and politics from Walter Clark, Josephus Daniels, Josiah Bailey, and others.

The Manuscripts Division of the Library of Congress contains some useful material. Unfortunately a fire destroyed the bulk of the Josephus Daniels Papers in 1913, and what remains is mostly family correspondence that rarely touches on politics. The Alexander J. McKelway Papers are relatively thin for the period. The Daniel A. Tompkins Papers supplement those in the Southern Historical Collection at Chapel Hill. The J. L. M. Curry Papers were also consulted.

The Walter Hines Page Papers in the Houghton Library of Harvard University proved to be of considerable value. This is a large collection which ranges over political as well as religious, cultural, and racial matters in the South and to a large extent in Page's native state, North Carolina. Page corresponded with a number of individuals figuring in this study.

Index

Adams, Charles F., 151
Adams, Herbert B., 89
Agricultural and Mechanical College, 22
Alderman, Edwin A., 8, 23, 32, 36, 81-86, 89-93, 132, 134-36
American Tobacco Company, 75, 79, 99-100, 105, 115, 118, 143, 151
Ammon, John, 55
Andrews, Alexander B., 99-100, 102, 107, 115-16
Angier, John C., 68
Asheville *Register,* 124
Atkins, David, 72-73
Atlanta *Constitution,* 41, 58
Aycock, Charles B., 1, 86, 90, 123, 133, 136-37, 139-40, 142, 156

Bailey, C. T., 28
Bailey, Josiah W., 37, 95, 102; ideology and politics of, 6-7, 78-80, 128-31, 133-34, 139-40, 157-59; and state aid, 28-29, 36, 78, 80-82, 84, 86, 127-29, 134, 157-58; and Daniels, 36-37, 141-43; and Kilgo, 78-80; and public schools, 87-89, 91-94, 132-37; and Clark-Kilgo controversy, 109; and Duke stock controversy, 119; and white supremacy, 127-31, 137; and deal with Simmons, 128-30; and race issue, 142-43; and Carr-Simmons contest, 145; and Bassett controversy, 153-54; and Massee controversy, 154-56; see also *Biblical Recorder*
Baptist Argus, 18
Baptists, 155; and state aid, 20-38, 78, 80-82, 84; and public schools, 26-27, 88, 90, 92-93; ideology and politics of, 37-38; racism of, 93-94; *see also* Protestants
Bassett, John S., 10-11, 63, 65, 68, 76, 89, 112, 121; controversy over racial views of, 146-56, 158

Biblical Recorder, 25, 28, 31-32, 36, 45, 78-80, 89, 92, 127-30, 134-36, 142-43, 148, 153, 155, 158; *see also* Bailey, Josiah W.
Bilbo, Theodore G., 142
Bishop, F. A., 51
Blair, H. M., 149, 156
Blanchard, C. W., 125
Brown, Joseph G., 102, 118, 146
Brown, William G., 68-69, 121, 150
Bryan, William J., 84, 96, 107, 112
Busbee, Fabius, 115
"Business Progressivism," *see* New South progressivism
Businessmen: and Democratic Party, 3, 98-101; and churches, 47-52; and Clark-Kilgo controversy, 115-16; and white supremacy, 122-23, 138-39; and Bassett controversy, 152
Butler, Marion, 33, 35, 39-40, 48, 83-86, 96, 107, 143

Cable, George W., 98
Cade, Baylus, 137
Cain, William, 30
Caldwell, Joseph P., 100, 103, 153, 155, 158; *see also* Charlotte *Observer*
Campbell, R. F., 125
Carr, Julian S., 68, 143-46
Cash, Wilbur J., 46, 151
Catawba College, 87
Charlotte *Observer,* 44, 56-57, 93, 109-10, 120, 125-26, 132, 128, 142, 158; and state aid, 31; on religion and politics, 36; and Populist criticism of churches, 41; on populistic preachers, 55; politics of, 99-101; and Kilgo, 103; and Clark-Kilgo controversy, 119; and Duke stock controversy, 119; and white supremacy, 122-23; and race issue, 141; and Bassett controversy, 152-53; and Bailey, 154-55; *see also* Caldwell, Joseph P.

University of North Carolina, 20-21; *see also* State aid

Vance, Zebulon B., 85
Vardaman, James K., 142

Waddell, Alfred M., 126
Wake Forest College, 21, 47, 89, 158
Washington, Booker T., 146
Watts, George W., 68
Webb, R. S., 75
Webster, John R., 104-6, 110-11, 115, 120, 137, 144-45, 152; *see also* Reidsville *Webster's Weekly*
Weeks, Stephen B., 11
Wesleyan Christian Advocate, 18
Western Christian Advocate, 73
Whitaker, J. B., 118
White, John E., 78, 82, 85, 87-88, 90, 127-28, 134-37, 143, 148

White supremacy campaigns, 122-40; *see also* Race
Wilmington, race riot in, 126
Wilmington *Messenger,* 30, 93, 98, 103-4, 123
Wilmington *Morning Star,* 98
Wilson, S. Otho, 32
Wilson, W. C., 120
Winston, George T., 21, 31-36, 81
Winston, Robert W., 11, 99, 112, 144
Winston *Sentinel,* 118
Winston *Union Republican,* 83, 130-31
Woodward, C. Vann, 4
World's Work, 12, 149, 152
Worth, W. H., 43

Yates, E. A., 44, 113
Young, James H., 35